CAMBRIDGE ENGLISH for schools

Student's Book One

ANDREW LITTLEJOHN & DIANA HICKS

CAMBRIDGE
UNIVERSITY PRESS

PUBLISHED BY THE PRESS SYNDICATE OF THE UNIVERSITY OF CAMBRIDGE
The Pitt Building, Trumpington Street, Cambridge, United Kingdom

CAMBRIDGE UNIVERSITY PRESS
The Edinburgh Building, Cambridge CB2 2RU, UK
40 West 20th Street, New York, NY 10011-4211, USA
10 Stamford Road, Oakleigh, VIC 3166, Australia
Ruiz de Alarcón 13, 28014 Madrid, Spain
Dock House, The Waterfront, Cape Town 8001, South Africa

http://www.cambridge.org

First Published 1996
New Look Reprinted 2001

Printed in the United Kingdom at the University Press, Cambridge

ISBN 0 521 42169 1 Student's Book
ISBN 0 521 42173 X Workbook
ISBN 0 521 42177 2 Teacher's Book
ISBN 0 521 42181 0 Class Cassette Set
ISBN 0 521 42130 6 Workbook Cassette

Contents

Map of Cambridge English for Schools 1

UNIT/TOPIC	GRAMMAR	VOCABULARY	SKILLS/STRATEGIES
1 Introduction Unit **Welcome to English**	'can', questions	Numbers, objects	Getting to know the book, classroom language
2 Test your English **Around the English-speaking world**	'be', personal pronouns, 'There is/are', negatives, 'have got'	Personal information, adjectives, countries, languages	Social phrases

Theme A A Parcel of English *Geography and Social studies* – maps, towns

3 Topic **Around our school**	'There is/are', 'be', Present simple	Places in a town, school subjects	Listening for information, writing a letter
4 Language focus **Present simple**	Present simple negative, parts of speech	Places on a map	Going shopping, asking for information
5 Activity **Making an exercise box**	Sentence structure	Vocabulary from Units 3–4	Making your own practice exercise
6 Culture matters **Life in the town**	Present simple	Places, descriptions	Reading for specific information, describing a place
7 Revision and evaluation **Units 3–6**	Grammar from Units 3–6	Vocabulary from Units 3–6	Self-assessment, thinking about learning
8 Special Unit **A Parcel of English**	Present simple	Describing the school, town and country	Making links with other students

Theme B The natural world *Biology* – animals and how they live; *Social studies* – uses of the countryside

9 Topic **In the wild**	Present simple questions, possessive adjectives	Types of animals, food, basic verbs	Listening and asking for information, describing
10 Language focus **Questions, possessives**	Present simple questions, possessive adjectives	Animals, social language	Asking for information, inviting
11 Activity **Animal posters**	Present simple	Descriptions of animals	Designing and writing a poster
12 Culture matters **Life in the countryside**	Present simple	Daily routines, leisure activities	Letter writing
13 Revision and evaluation **Units 9–12**	Grammar from Units 9–12	Vocabulary from Units 9–12	Self-assessment, thinking about learning

Theme C The way we live *Health education* – elements in good food

14 Topic **Food matters**	'some', 'any', object pronouns	Food, nutrition	Reading for detail, writing menus
15 Language focus **'some' and 'any', object pronouns**	'some', 'any', object pronouns	Recipes, personal interests	Talking about likes and dislikes
16 Activity **A questionnaire: how do they live?**	Present simple positive and question forms	Daily routines, opinions	Designing a survey, writing a report
17 Culture matters **Life at home**	Present simple	Types of houses, rooms	Reading and listening for detail
18 Revision and evaluation **Units14–17**	Grammar from Units 14–17	Vocabulary from Units 9–12	Self-assessment, designing your own test, thinking about learning

UNIT/TOPIC	GRAMMAR	VOCABULARY	SKILLS/STRATEGIES
Theme D Planet Earth *Music* – Holst's Planet Suite; *Science and Geography* – solar system, tides			
19 Topic **Into space**	Present continuous, comparisons	Basic action verbs, space and planets	Describing actions, asking questions, writing a postcard
20 Language focus **Present continuous, comparing**	Present continuous, comparisons	Eclipses, descriptions	Asking for travel information
21 Activity **Poems from the Earth and space**	Present simple and continuous	Space, Earth, stars	Brainstorming, writing poems
22 Culture matters **Life by the sea**	Present simple and continuous, 'There is/are'	The sea, leisure activities	Reading for detail
23 Revision and evaluation **Units 19–22**	Grammar from Units 19–22	Vocabulary from Units 19–22	Self-assessment, designing your own test, thinking about learning
Theme E Natural forces *Music* – Beethoven; *Science* – water cycle; *Geography* – seasons and weather			
24 Topic **The weather**	Frequency adverbs	Weather, months, processes	Describing processes
25 Language focus **Uncountables, comparing**	Countables and uncountables, comparisons, Present continuous for future reference	Weather, adjectives	Making plans with others
26 Activity **A poster: weather around the world**	Present simple (all forms), frequency adverbs	Weather around the world	Collecting and reporting information
27 Culture matters **Living with nature**	Present simple (all forms), comparisons, frequency adverbs	Seasons and free time activities	Reading poems
28 Revision and evaluation **Units 24–27**	Grammar from Units 24–27	Vocabulary from Units 24–27	Self-assessment, thinking about learning
Theme F Living history *History* – pre-history; *Social studies* – dangers today, celebrations			
29 Topic **The cavepeople**	'was/were', Past simple	Basic verbs, daily actions, adjectives	Brainstorming, making a poster
30 Language focus **Past simple**	'was/were', some regular and irregular past verbs	School life, cavepeople	Talking about past events
31 Activity **A book about your family and friends**	Past and present tenses	Family life	Collecting information, making a family tree
32 Culture matters **Living traditions**	Past and present tenses	Traditions and festivities	Reading for detail
33 Revision and evaluation **Units 29–32**	Grammar from Units 29–32	Vocabulary from Units 29–32	Self-assessment, designing your own test, writing to the authors
Theme Trail A revision game A game to revise the Topic and Language focus Units			

Unit ☐

Unit ☐

Unit ☐

Unit ☐

Unit ☐

Unit ☐

Unit ☐

Welcome to

CAMBRIDGE
ENGLISH
for schools
Student's Book One

A Parcel of English
What is it? Find out in Unit 8!

Unit ☐

Unit ☐

ner students.   4

3 It is very cold in
the sky. The
water vapour
becomes clouds.

Unit ☐

What's in *Cambridge English for Schools 1?*

Cambridge English for Schools 1 has three parts for you, the student.
There is a Student's Book, a Workbook and a Workbook Cassette.

Let's look at the Student's Book

1 Six Themes

This book has six Themes.
Match the letter to the name.
One name is not there. What is it?

Theme A   The natural world
Theme B   ....
Theme C   Living history
Theme D   The way we live
Theme E   A Parcel of English
Theme F   Natural forces

2 The Themes

Look through the book.
What can you learn about in *Cambridge English for Schools 1?*
Tell the class your ideas.

3 The Units

Look at the Units.
Find the missing pieces.
How are the Units
different?

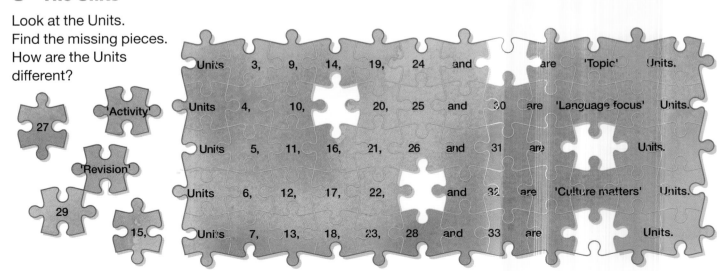

Units 3, 9, 14, 19, 24 and ___ are 'Topic' Units.
Units 4, 10, ___ 20, 25 and 30 are 'Language focus' Units.
Units 5, 11, 16, 21, 26 and 31 are ___ Units.
Units 6, 12, 17, 22, ___ and 32 are 'Culture matters' Units.
Units 7, 13, 18, 23, 28 and 33 are ___ Units.

27 'Activity'
'Revision'
29
15,

Let's look at the Workbook

4 Inside the Workbook

Look in the Workbook.
Find:

a listening exercise
a writing exercise
a reading exercise
a speaking exercise

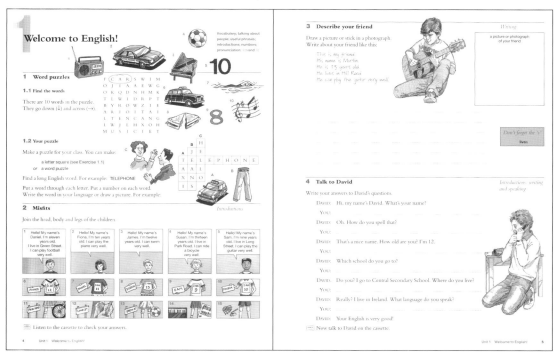

5 The Workbook Units

The Workbook also has six Themes. There are five Units in each one.
What are Units 6, 12, 17, 22, 27 and 32?

6 At the back

Look at the back of the Workbook. What is there?

Let's look at the Workbook Cassette

On the cassette, there are
the Workbook exercises.

There are songs from
the Student's Book.

7 Listen to the page numbers

The cassettes tell you the page numbers for the Units and the Exercises.

Listen. Find the Unit in the Student's Book or Workbook. Write your answers.

a Student's Book page .... is Unit ....
b Student's Book page .... is Unit ....
c Workbook page .... is Unit ....
d Workbook page .... is Unit ....
e Student's Book page .... is Unit ....
f Workbook page .... is Unit ....

1 Introductory Unit
Welcome to English

1 Vocabulary **You know a lot of English!**

Look at the pictures. Do you know the names in English?
Tell your teacher. What other English words or phrases do you know?

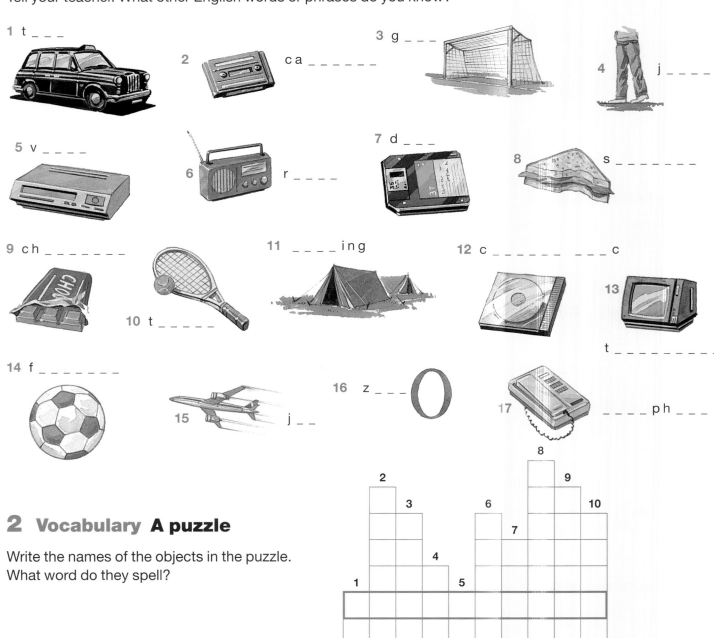

1 t _ _ _

2   c a _ _ _ _ _ _

3 g _ _ _

4   j _ _ _ _

5 v _ _ _ _

6   r _ _ _ _

7 d _ _ _

8   s _ _ _ _ _ _ _

9 ch _ _ _ _ _ _ _

10 t _ _ _ _ _

11 _ _ _ _ i n g

12 c _ _ _ _ _ _ _ _ _ c

13
t _ _ _ _ _ _ _ _ _

14 f _ _ _ _ _ _ _

15   j _ _

16   z _ _ _

17   _ _ _ _ p h _ _ _

2 Vocabulary **A puzzle**

Write the names of the objects in the puzzle.
What word do they spell?

3 Introductions Hello!

Listen to the cassette and look at the pictures.

Hello! My name is James.
I'm 12 years old.
I live in Hill Road.
I can swim very well.

Hello! My name is Martha.
I'm 13 years old.
I live in Park Road.
I can play football very well.

Who is who? Listen again.

James   Martha   Usha   Emma   Ali

I can **swim** very well.   I can **run** very well.   I can **sing** very well.   I can play football very well.   I can **draw** very well.

4 Numbers Talk about yourself

Tell the class about yourself.

Listen to the numbers and words.

10 ten   11 eleven   12 twelve   13 thirteen   14 fourteen   15 fifteen
I can ...   play the trumpet/piano/guitar very well.
             draw/run/play football/swim very well

5 Writing Make a poster

Draw a picture and write about yourself.
Sign it with your thumbprint!

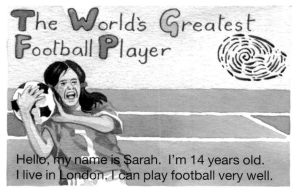

The World's Greatest Football Player

Hello, my name is Sarah. I'm 14 years old.
I live in London. I can play football very well.

6 Investigate Find out about your book

Work with your neighbour.

Look at the pictures on pages 6–7. Write the correct Unit number beside each picture.

Now look at pages 8–9 and do the exercises.

7 Classroom language **Some useful phrases**

Here are some phrases to help you learn English.
Write them in your language.

What's … in English?   What does … mean?
How do you spell …?   How do you say … in English?
I don't know.

Practise using the phrases. Ask your teacher some questions.

What does 'town' mean?

8 Numbers **What's the number?**

Can you say these numbers in English?

1   2   3   4   5   6   7   8   9   10   11   12   13   14   15   16   17   18   19   20

31   42   53   64   75   86   97   100

Draw a map of your class. Write a number in each place.
Ask your neighbour.

– *Who's in chair twenty?*
– *That's Steven. Who's in chair twelve?*
– *That's Isabel.*

> **Say it clearly!**
> 13: thir**teen**
> 14: four**teen**
> 30: **thir**ty
> 40: **for**ty

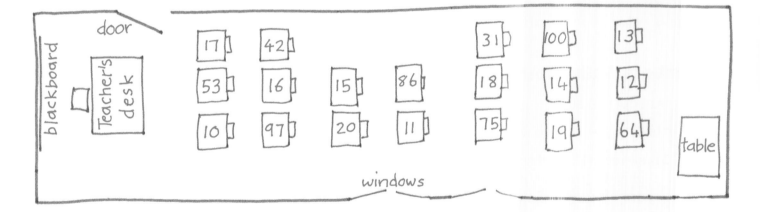

9 Sing a song! **I'm so happy**

Sing the song with your class.
The words are on page 154.

10 Review **Your Language Record**

Now complete your *Language Record*.

Language Record

Write the meanings of the words. Add the missing examples.

Word	Meaning	Example
who		
that		That's Isabel.
a name		My name is James.
a chair		
can		I can swim very well.
am		I am 12 years old.
am		I am English.
draw		
live		I live in Green Street.
play		I can play the piano.
play		I can play football.
run		
sing		

Classroom phrases

Write the meanings.

What's … in English? ....

What does … mean? ....

How do you spell …? ....

How do you say … in English? ....

I don't know. ....

1 'be' London to Dublin by boat

Circle the correct answer.
For example:

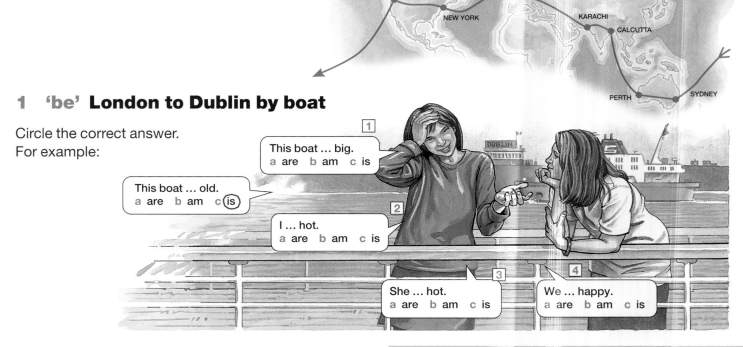

1 This boat ... big.
a are b am c is

This boat ... old.
a are b am c (is)

2 I ... hot.
a are b am c is

3 She ... hot.
a are b am c is

4 We ... happy.
a are b am c is

2 Personal details
Dublin to New York by plane

Complete the form about you.

JFK Airport Arrival Card

Name: .... First Language: ....

Address: .... Age: ....

.... Colour of hair: ....

Telephone number: .... Colour of eyes: ....

3 Pronouns New York to Vancouver by train

Circle the correct answer.

1 Where are ... going?
a you b they c it

2 ... are going to Vancouver.
a It b He c We

3 Is that train going to Vancouver?

No, ... isn't, it's going to Toronto.
a it b he c she

4 Where are ... going?
a he b they c it

I don't know

4 Social language **Vancouver to Sydney by submarine**

Circle the correct answer.

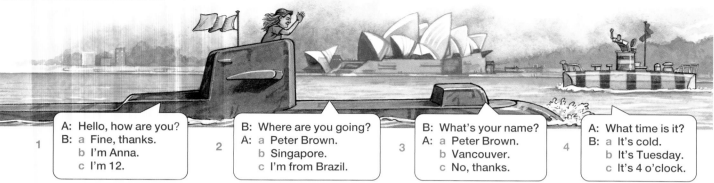

1 A: Hello, how are you?
   B: a Fine, thanks.
      b I'm Anna.
      c I'm 12.

2 B: Where are you going?
   A: a Peter Brown.
      b Singapore.
      c I'm from Brazil.

3 B: What's your name?
   A: a Peter Brown.
      b Vancouver.
      c No, thanks.

4 A: What time is it?
   B: a It's cold.
      b It's Tuesday.
      c It's 4 o'clock.

5 'There is/are' **Sydney to Perth by bus**

Circle the correct answer.

Let's have a quiz about Australia.

OK. Ask me some questions.

1 A: ... a lot of kangaroos in Australia?
      a Are there   b There are   c There is
   B: Yes!

2 A: ... an airport in Sydney. Right or wrong?
      a Is there   b There is   c There are
   B: Right!

3 A: ... a river in Perth?
      a Is there   b There are   c Are there
   B: Yes!

4 A: ... 17 million people in Australia. Right or wrong?
      a Is there   b There is   c There are
   B: Right!

6 Adjectives **Perth to Calcutta by ship**

Circle the correct answer.

1 A: Hello Peter, how are you?
   B: Fine, where are you?
   A: On the ship.
   B: Tell me about the ship.

   A: a It's a big ship.
      b It's a small ship.
      c It's a fat ship.

2 B: I can hear music.

   A: a Yes, it's modern music.
      b Yes, it's old music.
      c Yes, it's very cold music.

3 B: How is the captain?

   A: a He's very green.
      b He's very long.
      c He's very fat.

4 B: Is the weather nice?

   A: a Yes, it's very cold.
      b Yes, it's very hot.
      c Yes, it's very bad.

7 Negatives **Calcutta to Karachi by car**

Look at the pictures.
Circle the correct sentence.

1
a I haven't got a car.
b I'm not a car.
c This isn't a car.

2
a There isn't a house.
b Here, it isn't a house.
c I haven't got a house.

3
a He isn't old.
b We don't swim.
c I'm not rich.

4
a He isn't a dog.
b I can't find my dog.
c He doesn't sleep.

What's the problem?

8 'have/has got' **Karachi to London by helicopter**

Write four sentences. Use 'have got' and 'has got'.

John *has got a bag.*

Anna and Susan ....

Leo ....

Steven and Jack ....

Steven ....

Extension: extra practice
Around the world again

1 'be' You're in England. Get ready to go!

1.1 Listening Play a game to go around the world

Follow your teacher's instructions. If your teacher says 'You are …', do the actions. If your teacher says 'She is …', 'He is …', 'We are …' or 'They are …', don't do the actions.

1 in a boat

2 on a plane

3 on a train

4 in a submarine

chug chug

5 in a balloon

swoosh

6 in a car

7 in a helicopter

1.2 Writing Meet Martin Wilson

Listen to Martin.

Write sentences about yourself.
Say your sentences to the class.

Hello.

My name …

I am …

I am …

I live …

It is …

Hello. My name is Martin Wilson.
I'm English. I'm 12 years old.
I live in Liverpool. It's in England.

1.3 Writing In Liverpool

Read Martin's writing about Liverpool.

Write about your town in the same way.

> Liverpool is in the north west of England.
> It is on the River Mersey. It is a big city.
> About 500,000 people live here.
> Liverpool has got a very big port. It has
> also got an important football team.

2 Social language Stopover in America!

2.1 Listening Martin Wilson arrives in New York

Listen. Martin is at the airport in New York.
Complete the card.

JFK Airport Arrival Card

Name: _Martin Wilson_ First Language: ....

Address: _25, Long Street,_ Age: ....

Liverpool Colour of hair: ....

Telephone number: .... Colour of eyes: ....

2.2 Speaking Your personal information

Work in pairs. Find out about your partner.
Write the information on the card.

Welcome to New York. *And your first language is …*
Can you tell me … *What colour is …*
What's your … *What colour are … eyes?*
How old are you?

JFK Airport Arrival Card

Name: .... First Language: ....

Address: .... Age: ....

.... Colour of hair: ....

Telephone number: .... Colour of eyes: ....

2.3 Speaking Martin telephones his friends

Listen. Martin is talking to Sarah on the phone.

SARAH:	Hello.
MARTIN:	Hello! How are you?
SARAH:	Fine thanks. Where are you?
MARTIN:	I'm in Washington.
SARAH:	Where's Washington?
MARTIN:	It's in America.
SARAH:	In America!
MARTIN:	Yes, I've got friends here.
	They've got a big house.

In pairs, practise the conversation.
Choose other countries.

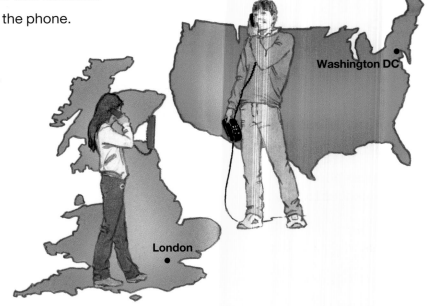

Washington DC

London

3 'There is/are' Stopover in Australia!

3.1 Speaking Martin sends his family a postcard

Can you label Martin's postcard?

a bridge   a port   a river

cars   trees   a park   houses

boats   tall buildings

What's in the picture? Tell the class.
You can use these words.

big old new beautiful small tall

There is a big …   There are a lot of …   There is an old …

3.2 Writing Write part of Martin's postcard

Complete Martin's postcard.
Use the words from Exercise 3.1.

3.3 Writing A postcard of your town

Find a postcard of your town or draw a picture.
Write about your town.

4 Negatives Stopover in India!

4.1 Reading India is very different from Australia

Read about India.

> India is a very big country. There are 850 million people there. The capital of India is New Delhi. There are 16 languages in India. There are elephants, lions and tigers. There are also very high mountains. India is in the Northern hemisphere. It is near China and Pakistan.

How is it different in Australia? Write some sentences.

There aren't 850 million people in Australia. There are 17 million.

Useful phrases: There isn't …   There aren't …   It isn't …   It hasn't got …

4.2 Play a game Is it true?

Work with a partner. Write four sentences about your country, town or school.
Make some sentences true and some false.

There isn't a train station here.   We haven't got tigers in our country.   It isn't very hot in our country.

Now work with your class in two teams. Say your sentences to the other team.
They say 'True' or 'False'. The first team to give 12 correct replies is the winner.

5 'have/has got' Stopover in Pakistan

5.1 Reading Meet some of Martin's friends in Pakistan

Here are some ways to describe your hair and eyes.

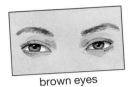
brown eyes

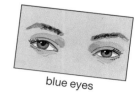
blue eyes

green eyes

curly hair

long hair

short hair

straight hair

Can you match these descriptions to the correct picture?

… are 13 years old. They've got short, curly hair and brown eyes.	… is 11 years old. He's got short, curly hair and green eyes.	… is 12 years old. He's got short, straight hair and brown eyes.

1
Ali

2
James

3
Fatma and Muneera

4
Jane

Listen and check your answers. One description is missing.
Can you describe that person?

5.2 Speaking Describe yourself

Work in a small group. Describe yourself to other students.

I'm 11 years old. I've got short, straight hair and brown eyes.

5.3 Speaking Arrrrgh!

You are in the mountains in Pakistan. Suddenly, you see a monster! Choose a picture and describe it to your group. They have to guess which monster it is.

1

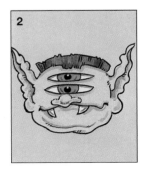
2

3

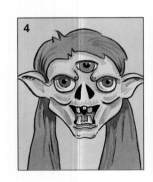
4

6 'be', 'have/has got' Welcome back to London!

6.1 Speaking Other places and other languages

Follow the lines.
Find the capital city
and the language.

Ask your partner:

   A: *Where is Tokyo?*
   B: *It's in Japan.*
   They speak Japanese there.

Think of some more cities
and ask your partner.

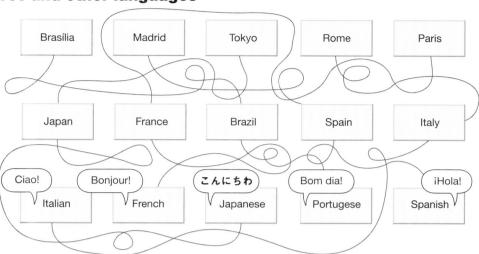

6.2 Listening Brasília has got a population of 1 million people

Listen. Choose list A or list B. Work with a partner and fill in the chart.

List A	Population
Brasília	*1 million*
Madrid	
Tokyo	

List B	Population
Rome	
Mexico City	
Paris	

Tell your partner your information, like this:

Brasília has got a population of 1 million.

6.3 Writing Write part of an encyclopaedia!

Read about Brasília.

Now choose two more cities and write
about them in the same way.

  Tokyo   Mexico City   Paris   Madrid   Rome

> ### *Brasília*
>
> Brasília is in Brazil. It has got a population of
> 1 million people and they speak Portuguese there.

7 Review Your Language Record

Now complete your *Language Record*.

Language Record

Adjectives Write the meanings. Add the missing examples.

Word	Meaning	Example
big		Liverpool is a big city.
small		
important		It has an important football team.
tall		There are many tall buildings.
beautiful		My town is very beautiful.
old		The houses are very old.
new		
long		My hair is very long.
short		

Pronouns Write the meanings.

Pronoun	Meaning	Pronoun	Meaning
I		we	
you		you	
he		they	
she			
it			

'be' Complete the table.

I'm (I am)
You're (you are)
He .... (............................)
She .... (............................)   English.
It .... (............................)   very old.
We .... (............................)
You .... (............................)
They .... (............................)

'have/has got' Complete the table.

I've got (have got)
You've got (have got)
He .... (.........................)
She .... (.........................)   curly hair.
It .... (.........................)   brown eyes.
We .... (.........................)
You .... (.........................)
They .... (.........................)

Useful phrases Write the meanings of these phrases.

How are you? ....   Can you tell me ....

Fine, thanks. ....   How old are you? ....

Where's ....   What's your address? ....

Theme A
A Parcel of English

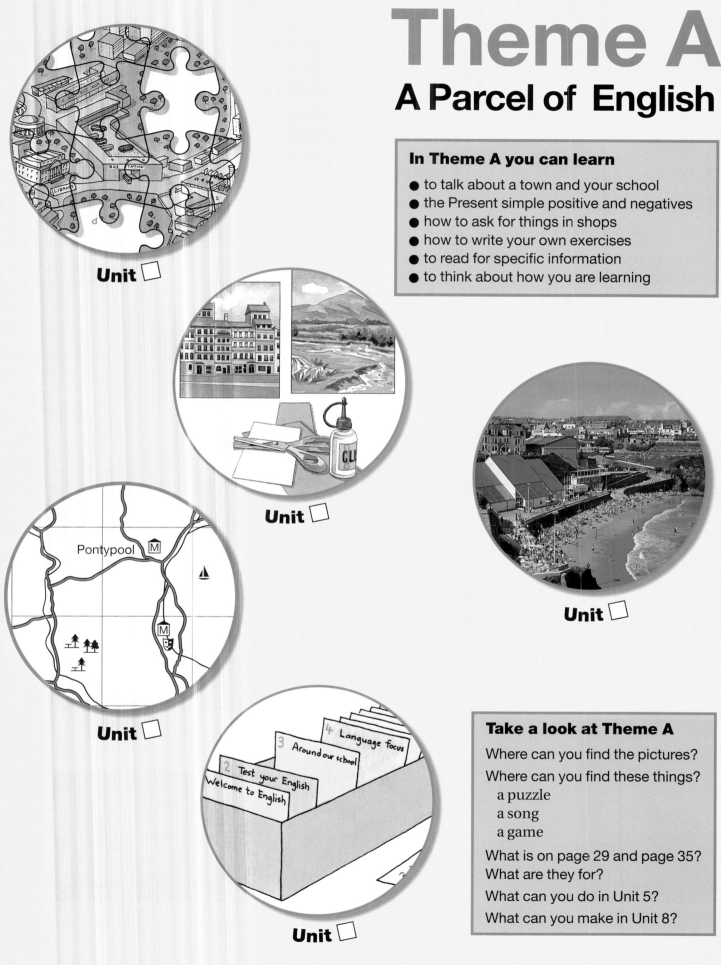

In Theme A you can learn
- to talk about a town and your school
- the Present simple positive and negatives
- how to ask for things in shops
- how to write your own exercises
- to read for specific information
- to think about how you are learning

Unit ☐

Unit ☐

Pontypool Ⓜ

Unit ☐

Unit ☐

Unit ☐

Take a look at Theme A

Where can you find the pictures?

Where can you find these things?
   a puzzle
   a song
   a game

What is on page 29 and page 35?
What are they for?

What can you do in Unit 5?

What can you make in Unit 8?

3 Topic Around our school

1 Your ideas **Where is your school?**

1.1 Discussion **Schools around the world**

Is your school in a town or in the country?

Look at the pictures. Does your school look like one of these?
Which schools do you think are in a town?
Which schools are in the country?

1.2 Vocabulary **Where you live**

Where do you live?
In the north?   In the east?
In the south?   In the west?

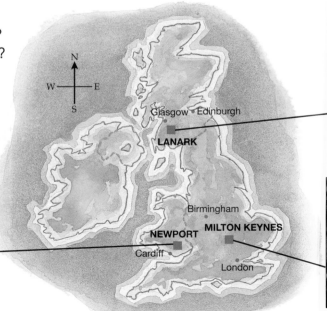

David lives in the north.

Anne and Pat live in the west.
They are friends.

Ali and Mona live in the south east.
They are brother and sister.

2 Vocabulary Near your school

Tell the class about the places near your school.

There is a park near our school.
There are some flats near our school.

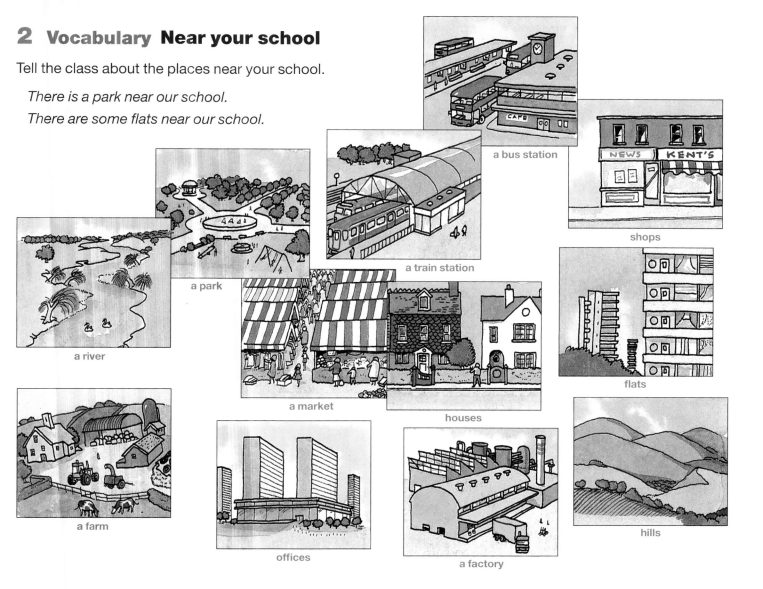

a bus station

shops

a train station

a park

flats

a river

a market

houses

a farm

offices

a factory

hills

3 Listening Where is it?

Listen to some sounds. Where are they from?
Write down your answers 1–6.

Check your answers with the class.

What's number 1?   It's a restaurant.   No, it's not. It's a …

4 Speaking Where am I?

Think of a place and mime it to the class.
They have to guess where you are.

You're in a market.
No, I'm not.

You're in a school.
No, I'm not.

You're in an office.
Yes, I am!

5 Reading Find the places

Here is a letter from Anne, in Newport. Work with a neighbour.
Read the letter and look at the puzzle.
Draw lines to show where each piece goes.

Compare your answers with other students in your class.

Listen to Anne's letter.

Clifton School
Newport
Gwent
Wales

Dear Everyone,
I don't live in England, I live in Wales!
Newport is a big town in the south
of Wales. It has got a population
of 120,000 people. My school is in
the north of the town. Near the
school there are shops, offices and
cafés.
A lot of students like football. After
school they play football in the park
near the sea. I don't like football. I
go to the swimming pool near the
bus station after school. I'm in the
school swimming team.

I live about four kilometres from
school. I don't walk to school. I
go on the school bus. There
are a lot of factories near
my flat. My mother works in one
of the factories. My father
doesn't work.
On Saturday mornings I have
guitar lessons in my teacher's
house near the library and
museum.
Write and tell me about your
town and school.

Love Anne

6 Listening **A favourite day**

Look at Mona and Ali's new school timetable. Do you do the same subjects?

📼 Listen and answer the questions. Compare your answers with other students.

What is Mona's favourite day?   What is her favourite subject?
What is Ali's favourite day?   What is his favourite subject?

	Lesson	Monday	Tuesday	Wednesday	Thursday	Friday
9.00	1	English	Maths	Science	English	Art
10.00	2	Geography	Maths	Religion	English	French
11.00		Break	Break	Break	Break	Break
11.30	3	Religion	Geography	English	Geography	Sports
12.30		Lunch	Lunch	Lunch	Lunch	Lunch
13.30	4	French	Science	Maths	Sports	French
14.30	5	History	History	History	Sports	Science

7 Speaking **Your favourite day**

Work with a partner. Look at your own timetable. Talk about your favourite day and favourite subject. Say your dialogue in front of the class.

Hi, do you like the timetable?
It's OK.
What's your favourite day?
It's …
We've got …
What's your favourite subject?
It's …
Do you like …
Yes, I do.
No, I don't.

8 Vocabulary **Make an exercise**

Can you join the parts to make seven words? What do they mean?

Find seven more words in this Unit. Make an exercise for your neighbour.

stat   time   sub   hist   reli   geog   fav

ion   ourite   table   ject   raphy   ory   gion

9 Sing a song **In my town, in the countryside**

📼 Sing the song with your class. The words are on page 154.

10 Decide ...

You can work by yourself, with a partner or in a small group.
Choose **Exercise 10.1** or **Exercise 10.2**. Or you can do something else.
Talk to your teacher and decide.

10.1 Speaking/Listening **A map game**

Copy this map. Put six more things on your map. Choose from this list.

a restaurant   a factory   a river   a market
a farm   a train station   a bus station   a park
some shops   some hills   some houses
some flats   some offices

Now work with a partner. Don't look at your partner's map. Tell him/her where your places are.

There is a school in the north east near the bus station.
There are some shops in the south west near the mountains.

Your partner can draw the places on his/her map. When you have finished, check.

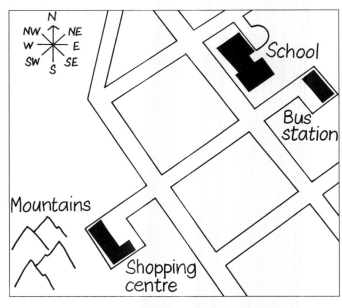

10.2 Writing **Write a letter to Anne**

Read Anne's letter in Exercise 5 again.
Write to Anne and tell her where you live.

Dear Anne,
Thanks for your letter. We live in ...... It is a .... It has got ...... Our school is .... There are .... near the school. In the street there are .... We haven't got .... near our school. We play ...... in ...... After school, I .....
    Best wishes,

11 Review **Your Language Record**

Now complete your *Language Record*.

Time to spare? Choose one of these exercises.

1 Look at Units 1 and 2 and make another word halves exercise (see Exercise 8 of this Unit).

2 Write your school timetable in English and put it in your exercise book.

3 Work with a partner. Play 'I spy' (= see) with the words in the Unit. For example:

A: I spy with my little eye   B: 'shops'?   B: 'school'?   B: 'some'?
  a word beginning with 's'.   A: No.   A: No.   A: Yes!

Language Record

Write the meanings. Add the missing examples.

Word	Meaning	Example
a break		We have a break at 10 o'clock.
a bus station		The bus station is near the park.
a factory		There is a car factory near the airport.
a farm		My brother has a farm.
a flat		
a hill		My school is on a hill.
a lesson		My favourite lesson is English.
a market		There is a market in the town centre.
a river		There is a river near my house.
a shop		
a subject		We have ten subjects at school.
a timetable		My timetable is in my English book.
a town		
a train station		The train station is in the town centre.
favourite		My favourite day is Friday.
much		I don't know much about Biology.
near		
small		
There are some		There are some shops near here.
go		
know		I know you.
learn		We learn about different things in school.
work		
live		

Choose some more words from this box. Add some examples and the meanings.

a park   a swimming pool   a museum   a library   a guitar   a bus   an office
north   south   west   east

4 Language focus
Present simple

1 Your ideas What's on the map?

1.1 Discussion Maps

Have you got a map of your town or country?
What can maps tell you? When can you use a map?

Tell the class your ideas.

1.2 Reading What can maps tell us?

Maps can tell us a lot. They can tell us about the places
we can visit. They can tell us about distances.
They can tell us where things are.

Here is a map of where Anne lives, in Newport.
Look at the map and answer these questions:

There is a castle in square D2. What's in square C4?
How big is the area? (Look at the scale and use a ruler!)
There are many picnic places. How many can you see?
Look at the symbols. What other things are there in
the area?

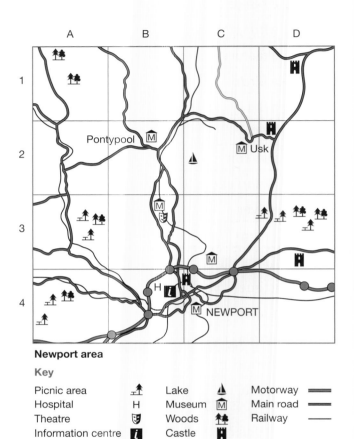

Newport area

Key

Picnic area		Lake	Motorway
Hospital	H	Museum M	Main road
Theatre		Woods	Railway
Information centre		Castle	

Scale 0   5   10
km

1.3 Writing Make a map

What places do you know in your area?
Make a list with the class.

Put a four squares by four squares box on
your blackboard. Mark on the roads, rivers,
railways and other important places.
Write the numbers and letters.

Write some sentences to describe your map.

There is a hospital in square A3.

The river goes from square A1 to D4.

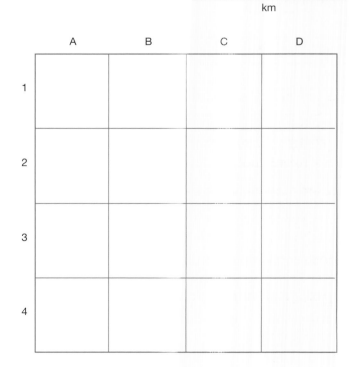

2 Grammar **Nouns, verbs and adjectives**

2.1 Parts of speech **What type of word is it?**

Nouns are the names of things. For example: a town   a road   a hospital

Verbs are action words. For example: go   start   walk

Adjectives describe something. For example: big   cold   hot

What do you call nouns, verbs and adjectives in your language? Can you think of examples in your language?

Draw three circles, like this:

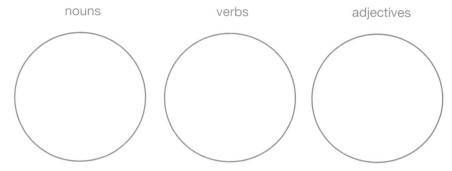

Now, with your neighbour,
put these words in the correct circle.

bicycle   dance   hot   history   good   country   river
swim   small   go   timetable   beautiful   map

Look at your *Language Records* from Units 1 and 3 and find more words to put in the circles. Compare your ideas with the rest of the class.

2.2 Practice **Play a game**

If your teacher says a noun, hold up your right hand. If your teacher says a verb, hold up your left hand. If your teacher says an adjective, shake your head.

3 Grammar **No, I don't!**

3.1 Present simple negative **Sentences with 'not'**

In Unit 2 there are sentences like this:

I haven't got a car.
We haven't got tigers in our country.
It isn't very hot in our country.

In Unit 3, there are more negative sentences like this:

I don't live in England. I don't walk to school.
I don't like football.
My father doesn't work.
I don't know.

How do you say these sentences in your language?

3.2 Negative form **Describe the negative**

How do you make negative sentences?
Write some more negative sentences in the tables.

Subject	+	....	+	....
I You We They		don't		know much about geography.

Subject	+	....	+	....
He She It		doesn't		have lunch at school.

3.3 Practice **What does your neighbour do?**

Find out three things that your neighbour
does and three things that he or she *doesn't* do.
You can use the verbs in the box.

Do you swim after school?   *Yes, I do.*
Do you play the piano?   *No, I don't.*

> play football   play the piano   like Maths
> play the guitar   live near an airport
> ride a bicycle   dance   paint   sing
> have breakfast before eight o'clock

Tell the class what you know about your neighbour. Remember the 's'.

David lives …   He doesn't …

> **Say it clearly!**
> likes   paints /s/
> lives   plays   has
> does /z/

3.4 More practice **Possible or impossible?**

Look at the map of Lanark, where David lives.
Are these sentences possible or impossible?

At the weekend …

1 David goes to the museum in Lanark.
   Possible! There is a museum in Lanark.

2 David goes by train to Rosebank.
   Impossible! David doesn't go by train.
   There isn't a train station in Rosebank.

3 David swims in the sea near Lanark.

4 David swims in the river near Lanark.

5 David rides his bicycle to Carstairs.

6 David visits lots of picnic places near Lanark.

7 David looks at the planes at the airport in Lanark.

8 David walks to the castle.

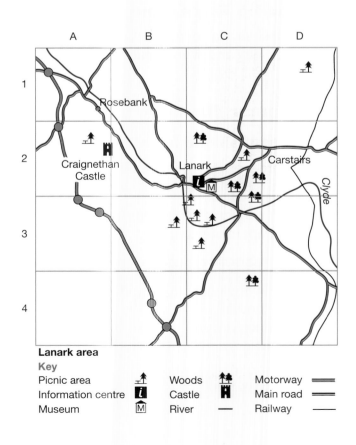

Lanark area
Key
Picnic area — Woods — Motorway
Information centre — Castle — Main road
Museum — River — Railway

Out and about with English

4 Language functions Going shopping

4.1 Your ideas Pocket money

Do you have pocket money? What do you do with it?

4.2 Asking for information Mona and Ali go shopping

 Listen. What do Mona and Ali want to buy?

MONA: Look, Ali. Here's a cassette of my favourite band. Excuse me, how much is this cassette?
MAN: That's £9.20.
ALI: That's expensive. Let's try another shop.

MONA: Here it is, Ali. Excuse me, can I have that cassette, please?
WOMAN: Here you are. That's £7.40, please.
MONA: Thank you. What do you want, Ali?
ALI: Some computer games and a computer magazine. Let's go to the newsagent's.
MONA: Good. I can get a box of chocolates for Mum there.

ALI: Can I pay for this computer game and magazine, please?
WOMAN: The game is free with the magazine.
ALI: Great!
MONA: Can I have that box of chocolates, please?
WOMAN: Yes, of course. That's £4.75 and £2.50. That's £7.25, please.
ALI: Thanks.

4.3 Practice **In a shop**

Now you try it. Work with a partner. You are in a shop.
You can change the conversation.

Excuse me, how much is this …?
How much are these …?
Can I have that …, please?
Can I pay for these …, please?

That's …, please.
Here you are.
Yes, of course.

Act out your dialogue for the class.

£10.50

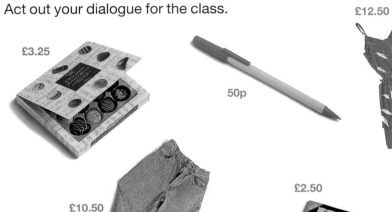
£3.25

50p

£12.50

25p

£5.50

£10.50

£2.50

£15.25

£2.50

5 Review **Your Language Record**

Now complete your *Language Record*.

Time to spare? Choose one of these exercises?

1 Use the *Ideas list* on pages 150–151 to make an exercise for another student.

2 How many subjects can you find in this puzzle? The words go down (↓) and across (→). What word can you make with the letters which are like this?

3 Make a list of some towns, mountains and rivers in your country. Write some sentences about where they are. For example:

   Mount Everest is in the north.
   The River Amazon is in the south.

E	N	G	L	I	S	H	S	E	G
H	M	A	T	H	S	A	R	T	E
I	S	D	S	P	O	R	T	Z	O
S	C	G	U	I	D	E	C	F	G
T	I	B	G	M	Y	D	S	Z	R
O	E	K	I	U	T	R	E	D	A
R	N	G	T	S	I	P	N	J	P
Y	C	G	T	I	U	I	J	G	H
M	U	S	I	C	F	R	T	D	Y

Language Record

Going shopping Write the meanings.

How much is this? How much are these? ....

Excuse me, can I have … please? ....

I want to buy ....

Here you are. ....

Can I pay for these? ....

That's ....

Yes, of course. ....

Present simple negative Complete the table. Write some more examples.

Pronoun	don't/doesn't	Verb phrase	Pronoun	don't/doesn't	Verb phrase
I	don't	have Maths on Friday.	We		
You	don't	eat lunch at home.	They		
He/She/It					

Present simple Write some more examples.

Pronoun	Verb phrase	Pronoun	Verb phrase
I	have got long hair.	We	go to school by bus.
You	live in a flat.	They	play
He	has got long hair.		
She	lives in a flat.		
It			

Learn more about your book!

1 Look at the back of the book

Look at pages 150 to 159.
Complete the list of sections.
  Ideas list
  Useful sets

....

....

....

What can you do with each section?
Tell the class your ideas.

2 Look at the sections

Where can you find
  a the days of the week?
  b a map of Brazil?
  c an example of an exercise?
  d the words from the book?
  e a list of numbers ?
  f the capital of Italy ?
  g the names of the seasons?
  h which words are nouns
     or verbs?
  i something to sing?

3 Look at the Wordlist/Index

In which Units are these words?
Are they nouns, verbs or adjectives?
  rise ☐   rain ☐
    tall ☐   elephant ☐
In which Unit(s) can you learn about
  possessive adjectives? ☐
  Present simple questions? ☐
  asking for information? ☐
  making plans? ☐

5 Activity
Making an Exercise Box

Writing exercises helps you learn English. In this Unit you can make a box of exercises for other students to do.

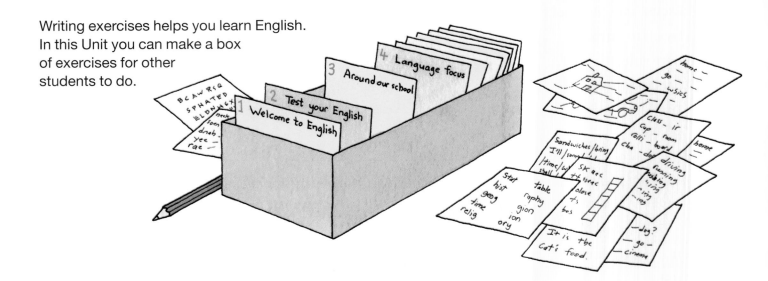

Before your lesson

Step 1 Look back

Look through Units 1, 2, 3 and 4. Write down on which page there is:

    a vocabulary exercise   a listening exercise   a reading exercise   a writing exercise

---

In your lesson

Step 2 Types of exercise

Show your neighbour which exercises you found. How many different kinds of exercises can you find?

Step 3 The Ideas list

Here are three types of exercises.

1 Word halves

2 A word puzzle

E	N	G	L	I	S	H	S	E	G
H	M	A	T	H	S	A	R	T	E
I	S	D	S	P	O	R	T	Z	O
S	C	G	U	I	D	E	C	F	G
T	I	B	G	M	Y	D	S	Z	R
O	E	K	I	U	T	R	E	D	A
R	N	G	T	S	I	P	N	J	P
Y	C	G	T	I	U	I	J	G	H
M	E	S	I	C	F	R	T	D	Y

3 Mixed-up sentences

1 I very can play well football

2 a factory near school our There is

3 are ? How you

Can you find the same types of exercises in the *Ideas list* on pages 150–151?

Work in a small group. Make up some exercises for other students to do.

Word halves: find 12 new words and divide them. Mix them up. Write the meaning in your language or draw a small picture.

Word puzzle: choose eight words and put them in a letter square.

Mixed-up sentences: find eight sentences. Mix up the words.

Write a title for the exercises (for example, *Word halves*) and put your name on it. Write the answers on the back of the paper. Put the exercises in the box.

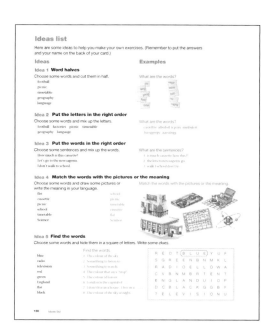

Step 4 Take an exercise

Take an exercise from the box. See if you can do it. Don't write on the paper! You can check your answers on the back.

Step 5 How you learn: evaluation

Discuss these questions with the people in the class.

Is it difficult to write exercises?
Were the exercises in the box easy to understand?
How can you write better exercises next time?

6 Culture matters
Life in the town

a new town

1 Your ideas **About your country**

Look at the pictures in this Unit.
Are there towns like these in your
country? Where are they?
Share your ideas with the class.

a farming town

a seaside town

an industrial town

2 Deducing **British towns**

Look at the map. Work with a partner.
Where do you think the pictures
in Exercise 1 are from?

Find these towns:

Newport
Wick
Newquay
Milton Keynes

What type of town
is each one, do
you think?

an industrial town
a farming town
a new town
a seaside town

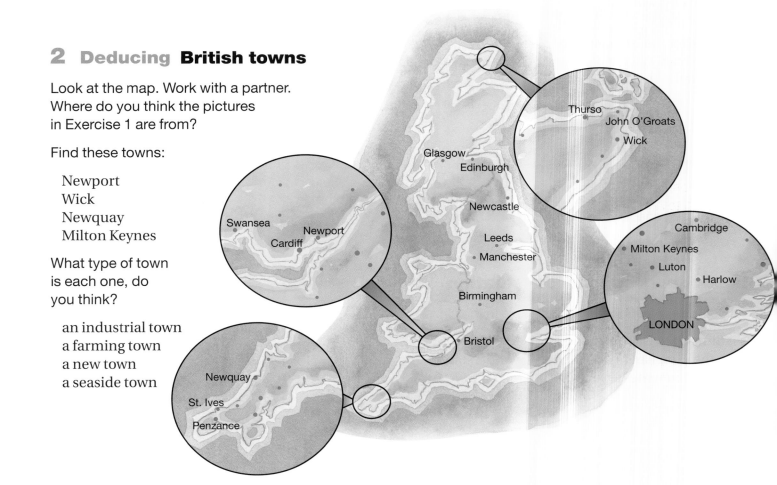

Thurso
John O'Groats
Wick
Glasgow
Edinburgh
Newcastle
Leeds
Manchester
Swansea
Newport
Cardiff
Cambridge
Milton Keynes
Luton
Harlow
Birmingham
LONDON
Bristol
Newquay
St. Ives
Penzance

3 Reading **Are you right?**

Read these texts to check your answers.

🖭 You can hear the texts on the cassette.

THE WELSH TOURIST BOARD

There are many big industrial towns in
South Wales. They make different things.
Near Newport, there are old coal mines.
They make steel there.

ENGLISH
TOURIST BOARD

*Near London there
are many new towns.
Milton Keynes is a new
town. There are new
flats, new houses, new
shops, new factories
and new offices in
the new towns.*

*In the south west
of England there are
many seaside towns.
People go there on
holiday. Newquay,
Penzance and St Ives
are all examples of
holiday towns.*

THE *Scottish* TOURIST BOARD

Scotland has many
small farming towns in
the north like Wick. They
have sheep and cows.
Every Wednesday there
is a big animal market
in the farming towns.

4 Reading **Where are the postcards from?**

Read the postcards and choose the correct postmark for each one.

🖭 Listen to Alex, Simon and Rita read their postcards.

MILTON KEYNES
26 JUL 1996
8- 30 PM

WICK
19 AUG 1996
9- 05 PM

NEWPORT
08 AUG 1996
8- 15 PM

Hi!
I'm on holiday in _____
The farming villages on this
postcard are near my aunt's
house. She lives in a very
old village. Her house is
white and it has got small
windows. Farmers live in
the cottages and there are
animals in their gardens.
See you soon,
Love Alex

Hello everyone!
I am in _____
It's an industrial town in South
Wales. My friends here live in
a small house in a terraced
street.
We play football in the small
streets. People work in the
factories and the mines here
They make cars and steel.
It's very different from where
I live.
Love to you all,
Simon

Dear All,
I am on holiday in ____
This town has got new offices,
new factories and new
schools. People live in new
flats and houses. In the
morning a lot of people
go to work in the new
offices. There are parks
and there is a big
shopping centre. I like
it here.
See you at the weekend,
Love Rita

7 Revision and evaluation
Units 3–6

1 Self-assessment How well do you know it?

How well do you think you know
the English you learned in Units 3–6?
Put a tick (✓) in the table.

Now choose some sections to revise
and practise.

	very well	OK	a little
Say what is in a town			
Present simple negatives ('doesn't/don't')			
Talk about school subjects			
New words			
Going shopping			

2 There is/are Say what's in a town

What's in this town?
Write some sentences.

There are some shops
near the bus station.
There is a bank near
the park.

3 Present simple negatives What do they do?

Write about the students.

	Question	Yes	No
🎹	1 Do you play the piano?	✓	✓✓✓✓✓✓✓
🏐	2 Do you play football?	✓✓✓✓✓✓✓	✓
🏢	3 Do you live in a flat?	✓✓✓✓✓	✓✓
🧪	4 Do you like Science?	✓✓✓✓✓✓	✓
🐎	5 Do you ride a horse?	✓	✓✓✓✓✓✓
🚶	6 Do you walk to school?	✓✓✓✓✓✓	✓
📖	7 Do you go to the library?	✓✓✓	✓✓✓✓✓

1 One student plays the piano. Seven students don't play the piano.

2 Seven students .... One student doesn't ....

3 ....

4 ....

5 ....

6 ....

7 ....

4 School subjects **A problem to solve**

Read the sentences and complete the timetable.

The students have two free lessons. When are they?
Compare your answers with other students.

Lesson	MONDAY	TUESDAY	WEDNESDAY	THURSDAY	FRIDAY
1	Maths				
2		Maths			
3			Maths		
	Lunch	Lunch	Lunch	Lunch	Lunch
4				Maths	Maths
5					
6					

- On Friday, the students have two lessons of Science after lunch. They don't have Science on Wednesday and Thursday but they do have it in Lesson 6 on Monday and Tuesday.
- The Geography teacher doesn't come on Tuesday. She comes in for Lesson 2 on other days.
- They don't have English on Monday. They have it before Geography on other days.
- They play Sport for two lessons on Thursday after lunch.
- The History teacher doesn't come on Thursday and Friday. He comes after lunch on other days.
- The Music teacher doesn't come on Monday or Wednesday. He teaches before lunch on other days.
- The Language teacher doesn't come on Thursday or Friday. She teaches two lessons of Language on Wednesday and one lesson of Language on the other days, after lunch.

5 Vocabulary **New words**

How many of these places can you find in the word square?
They go across and down.

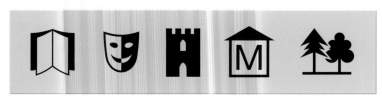

L	P	A	T	T	W	C	L
I	Y	N	B	H	O	A	E
B	M	U	S	E	U	M	C
R	U	S	V	A	G	T	A
A	C	I	M	T	O	O	S
R	Y	H	E	R	H	D	T
Y	L	U	S	E	A	W	L
A	W	O	O	D	S	P	E

Make another word puzzle for other students.

6 Going shopping Who says what?

Look at the pictures. Choose the
correct sentences for each picture.

1 Here you are.
2 Bye.
3 Can I have that bag, please?
4 That's £9.40.
5 Bye.
6 That's £8.
7 Thanks. £2 change.
8 That's expensive! How much
   is that?
9 Thanks. Here you are. £10.
10 Excuse me, how much is
   this, please?

Listen and check
your answers.

7 Self-assessment Were you right?

Look back at the chart in Exercise 1. Were you right?

8 How you learn Evaluation

8.1 Discussion Talk about your English work

First, with your class, decide which groups will look at Unit 3 or Unit 4 or Units 5 and 6.

Then work in a group of three or four students. Decide who will report back to the class.
Look through the Units you chose and talk about these questions:

Which exercises were easy?
Which exercises were difficult?
Which exercises were useful?

Tell the rest of your class what your group said.

8.2 Your own ideas Easy or difficult?

Draw a line like this one and write some Unit and
Exercise numbers on it. Give your paper to your teacher at
the end of the lesson. (You don't need to put your name on it.)

You can also write something (in your language) about your English
lessons for your teacher to read.

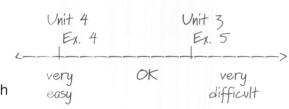

8 Special Unit
A Parcel of English

Before your lesson

1 Getting ready Pictures of you and your town

Draw a small picture of yourself
(5cm × 5cm) or find a passport photo.
Find some postcards and photographs
of your town to take to your lesson.

You also need glue, scissors and small
pieces of paper.

In your lesson

2 Discussion A Parcel of English

Look at the picture of a Parcel of English on page 7. Discuss these questions with your class.

What is in the parcel?
What can you do with your parcel?
Can you display it in your school?
Can you give it to a class in your school or send it to a school in another country?

3 Your ideas What's in the Parcel of English?

What can you put in your Parcel of English? With your class, make a list of your ideas.
(If you want to post your Parcel of English, remember that it can't be very big!)

You and your class   Your school   Your town
photographs   timetables   postcards

4 Writing A picture and description of me

For the first part of your Parcel of English, you can
write a short description of yourself. For example:

My name is ... . I am ... old.
I've got ... . I like ... and I can ... .

Look at Unit 1 Exercise 4 for help.

Put your picture on the small piece of paper from
your teacher. Write your description next to it.

Your teacher will put all your descriptions together.

5 Writing a draft Writing in groups

Divide into groups of three or four students. First, with your class decide which part of the Parcel of English (a–d) each group will write.

Your town

a Where people work
b Where people go in their free time

Your school

c A description of your school
d The subjects and timetable

 Listen to these examples.

About our town

Where people work in our town

In our town, people work in car factories. They make cars. Some people work in shops in the city centre and some people work in hotels. A lot of people work at the airport.

Where people go in their free time

In our town, people go to the cinema in their free time at weekends. Some people go dancing. Many people do sports — football, swimming, and bicycle riding. A lot of people go to restaurants and cafés.

About our school

A description of our school

Our school is in the north of the city near the airport and factories. It is very big. There are 40 rooms and 700 students in the school. We've got a football field, three laboratories and a computer room. Our classroom is near the computer room.

Our school day

We go to school six days a week. We start lessons at 8 o'clock and we go home at 3 o'clock. We have lunch from 12 o'clock to 1 o'clock. We have 8 lessons every day. One lesson is 40 minutes. The students come to school when they are 11 years old.

Work in your group. Read the examples again. Talk about and write your part of the parcel. Help each other with words and spellings. (Everybody in your group must write.)

6 Finalising Put it together

Now put your work on a piece of paper with your pictures. If you have time, you can write about the pictures.

7 More ideas Your Parcel of English!

Look at Exercise 3 again. For your next lesson, bring more things for your Parcel of English. Put them with your pictures and writing.

You now have a Parcel of English to send to another school!

Unit ☐

This is a Monarch butterfly. It is very beautiful. It lives in ~~anada, the United States and~~ lives for about nine mon~~ leaves. In the~~

Unit ☐

Unit ☐

~~uffes~~
giraffes sleep?
hippopotamus
?
Where do p~~
How many
a tarantula
eat meat?

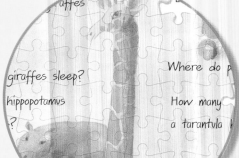

Unit ☐

Unit ☐

Theme B
The natural world

In Theme B you can learn

● to talk about animals and how they live
● Present simple questions
● possessive adjectives
● how to invite someone
● how to write a poster about animals
● to read and listen for specific information
● to think about how you are learning

Take a look at Theme B

Where can you find the pictures?

Where can you find these things?
  a graph
  a song
  a letter

What can you do in Unit 11?

What can you learn in Unit 12?

9 Topic In the wild

1 Vocabulary What is it?

With your neighbour, write the correct letter by each word.

- ☐ a kangaroo
- ☐ an elephant
- ☐ a parrot
- ☐ a whale
- ☐ a crocodile
- ☐ a shark
- ☐ a bee
- ☐ a monkey

2 Listening Buzzz ...

🔊 Listen to some animal sounds. Which animals are they? Write a number in each picture.

Tell the class your ideas.

What's number two?

I think it's a horse.

I don't think so. I think it's a cow.

3 Reading Mammals, reptiles, insects, birds and fish

There are many types of animals. Match the two halves of each definition.

Compare answers with your neighbour. Then listen and check.

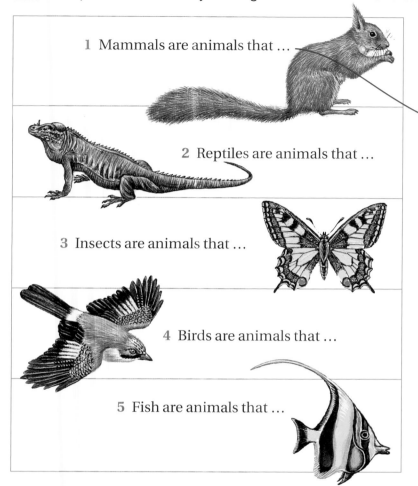

1 Mammals are animals that …

2 Reptiles are animals that …

3 Insects are animals that …

4 Birds are animals that …

5 Fish are animals that …

a … lay eggs. Many of them can fly. Their blood is warm.

b … give milk to their babies. They have got warm blood.

c … have got cold blood. They all lay eggs and their skin is thick.

d … live in water. Their blood is cold.

e … have got six legs. Most of them have got wings and can fly.

Look at the animals in Exercises 1 and 2. Are they mammals, reptiles, insects, birds or fish? Tell the class what you think.

4 Reading What are we?

People are also a type of animal. Are these sentences true (√) or false (×)?

a We give milk to our babies. ☐
b We live in water. ☐
c Our skin is thick. ☐
d We lay eggs. ☐
e Our blood is warm. ☐
f We have six legs. ☐

What type of animal are we?

5 Sing a song Wimoweh

Sing the song with your class.
The words are on page 154.

6 Graphic information How do they live?

Here is some more information about animals.
Look through the information and find an animal that

- **a** sleeps for eight hours at night.
- **b** lives for twenty years.
- **c** eats insects and fruit.
- **d** eats grass and sleeps for five hours.

**How many hours
do they sleep?**

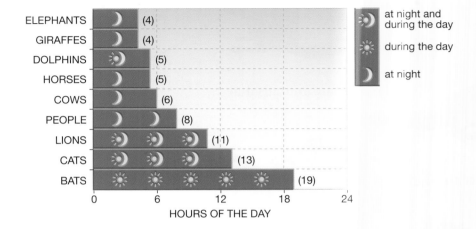

HOURS OF THE DAY

How long do they live?

people	elephants	dolphins	horses	cows	lions	giraffes	cats	bats
75 years	60 years	50 years	25 years	20 years	20 years	20 years	15 years	5 years

What do they eat?

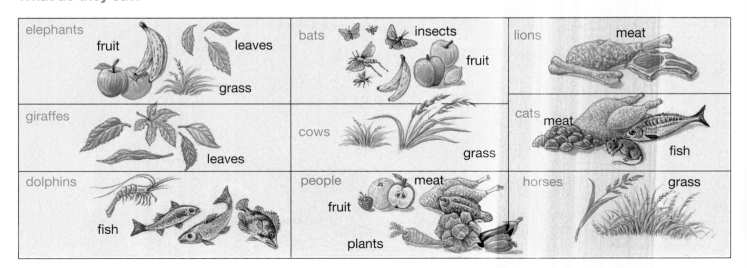

7 Practice **Ask about the animals**

Now, in pairs, ask each other about the animals.

What do elephants eat?
How long do lions live?
How many hours do cats sleep?

They eat fruit, leaves and grass.
They live for 20 years.
They sleep for 13 hours.

8 Listening **Which animal is it?**

🔲 Listen to part of a radio programme about animals.
Which animal are they talking about?

9 Speaking **Your own radio programme**

Imagine you are a famous explorer. You have discovered a
very strange animal. Draw a picture of the animal and complete
the report. Give the animal a name.

ANIMAL REPORT

Name of animal:

What does it look like?
It's got ...

What does it eat?

How many hours does it sleep?

Where does it live?

How long does it live?

Now imagine that you are on the radio. With your neighbour, prepare
a radio interview. You can use the questions to help you.
Act out your interview for the class.

10 Decide …

You can work by yourself, with a partner or in a small group.
Choose **Exercise 10.1** or **Exercise 10.2**. Or you can do **something else**.
Talk to your teacher and decide.
You can use the *Ideas list* on pages 150–151 to make an exercise.

10.1 Asking questions **A game about some animals**

One person thinks of an animal. The other people ask questions to find out the
name of the animal. The person can only say 'Yes, it is/does' or
'No, it isn't/doesn't'.

Take turns to think of an animal.

Does it …

live in Africa?   eat meat?   eat insects?
live for 20 years?   sleep a lot?

Is it …

a mammal?   a reptile?   an insect?   a bird?
a fish?   very big?   very small?

10.2 Writing **Write about some animals**

Read this description. Which animal is it?

Now write about three animals. Give your
descriptions to some other students.
Can they guess which animals they are?

> This animal is a mammal
> and lives in Africa. It sleeps
> four hours a day and it
> doesn't eat meat. It lives
> for about 20 years.

11 Review **Your Language Record**

Now complete your *Language Record*.

Time to spare? Choose one of these exercises.

1 Choose an exercise from your class *Exercise Box* or use the *Ideas list* on pages
150–151 to make an exercise for the *Exercise Box*.

2 Think of an animal and write a dialogue like the one in Exercise 10.1. Write the
name of the animal on the back. Give it to another student to read and guess.

3 Imagine … You are on another planet. You can see a strange animal. What is it?
Draw a picture and write a description. (See Exercise 9.)

Language Record

Write the meanings. Add the missing examples.

Word	Meaning	Example
a mammal		A whale is a mammal.
a bird		There is a bird in the tree.
a fish, fish		Do you like fish?
a baby, babies		Mammals give their babies milk.
a leg		Insects have six legs.
an insect		Bees are insects.
an egg		Birds lay eggs.
milk		Baby whales drink milk.
water		Fish live in water.
meat		
blood		Reptiles have cold blood.
people		
fruit		
warm		Our blood is warm.
cold		It is very cold today.
(to) sleep		Bats sleep during the day.
at night		Elephants sleep at night.
during the day		Bats sleep during the day.
How long …?		
What …?		
When …?		
How many …?		

Choose some more words from this box. Add their meanings and examples.

> a kangaroo   a parrot   a whale   a crocodile   a shark   a bee   a monkey   a cow
>
> a sheep   a dolphin   a lion   a giraffe   a bat   to fly   to lay   skin   thick   a wing

10 Language focus
Questions, possessives

1 Your ideas **Some more animals**

Here are some more animals.
What do you know about them?
Tell your class your ideas.

● Where do they live?

in trees   in rivers
underground   by the sea …

● What do they eat?

insects   plants
mammals   fish …

● Where in the world do they live?

in Asia   Africa   Europe
Antarctica   India   Australia
North America   South America

A panda ➤

A humming bird ▲

▼ A hippopotamus

▼ A tarantula

2 Listening **Which animal is it?**

Anne and her friend Pat are looking at the photographs in
Exercise 1. Listen. Which animal are they talking about?

ANNE: Gosh! How beautiful!
PAT: Yes, it is.
ANNE: Where do they live?
PAT: In trees, of course.
ANNE: I know that! I mean where
in the world do they live?
PAT: Oh sorry. Well, they live in
North America and South America.
Countries like Mexico and Brazil.
ANNE: How do they fly like that?
PAT: Well, they move their wings very fast.
They drink nectar from flowers.
ANNE: Oh. You're clever. How do you know
all this?
PAT: I've got this magazine at home!
ANNE: Oh!

3 Grammar Asking questions

3.1 Meaning Types of questions

In Units 3–7, there were questions with the verb 'be' ('am/is/are'). Like this:

Where is the airport?   Where are the factories?

In this Unit and Unit 9, there are questions with 'do' or 'does'. Like this:

What does it eat?   Do insects sleep?   How long do lions live?

Look at Units 1–9 again. Find some more questions with 'do' or 'does'.
Write down five or six examples. What do they mean in your language?

3.2 Question form Describe the questions

Look at your examples and complete the
description. Make notes about Present
simple questions. Where is the verb?
Where is the subject?

Tell the class about your ideas.

Present simple questions

Do   + ...

Does   + ...

+ .... ?

Notes

3.3 Some more practice Meaning and form

Work with a partner and do
Exercises **A**, **B** and **C**.

A Which piece goes where?
Choose the correct piece 1–8
for each space A–H.

How   A   do giraffes sleep?

B   do pandas eat?

C   do giraffes sleep?

Does a hippopotamus   F   eggs?

Where do pandas   D

How many   E   does a tarantula have?

G   a hippopotamus eat meat?

H   tarantulas eat people?

1 lay
2 live?
3 Does
4 When
5 Do
6 long
7 legs
8 What

B Write a question for each answer.

How long do giraffes sleep?   They sleep about four hours a day.

They sleep at night.   They eat bamboo.   They live in China.   No, it doesn't. It eats grass.
No! It's a mammal.   It has eight legs.   No, they don't. But they bite people!

C Look at Unit 9, Exercise 6 and write four more questions about animals. Ask other students to write their answers. You can use these words:

How long …?   How many …?   What …?   Where …?
When …?   Do …?   Does …?

How long do dolphins sleep?

Dolphins sleep for five hours.

What type of animals have cold blood?

Reptiles have cold blood.

4 Grammar 'my, your, his, her' …

4.1 Possessive adjectives **What do you say?**

How do you say these sentences in your language?

Our skin is thick.

Snakes are reptiles, too. Their blood is cold.

A cow gives milk to its babies.

You move your wings very fast.

Words like 'their', 'its', 'your', and 'our' are called *possessive adjectives*. Other possessives are 'my', 'his' and 'her'. In English, there are different possessive adjectives for each person.

Step 3 Write about your pictures

In your group, write about your pictures. Stick your pictures on your poster paper.

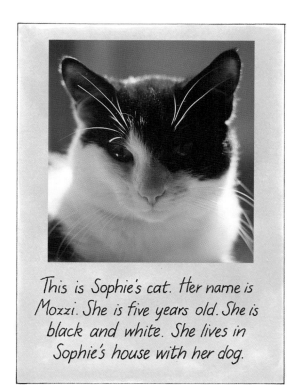

This is Sophie's cat. Her name is Mozzi. She is five years old. She is black and white. She lives in Sophie's house with her dog.

This is a Monarch butterfly. It is very beautiful. It lives in Canada, the United States and Mexico. It lives for about nine months. It eats leaves. In the winter it goes from Canada to Mexico.

Step 4 Talk about your posters

When you are ready, put your posters on the wall of your class. Go and look at the other posters. Talk about what is on the posters.

This is a hippopotamus. The hippopotamus is a very strange animal. It is very fat and heavy. It has a very thick skin. It lives in Africa and it eats grass.

Step 5 How you learn: Evaluation

Discuss your poster with the people in your class.

Was it easy or difficult to do the posters? Why?
Was it easy or difficult to work in your group? Why?
How can you do it better next time?

12 Culture matters
Life in the countryside

1 Your ideas About your country

What types of farms are there in your country? Do people go to the countryside in their free time? What do people do there?

Look at the photograph. Does your countryside look like this?

2 Listening Working in the country

Farming is very important in Britain. In the north, there are a lot of sheep farms. In the south west, a lot of farms produce milk and in the south east, they produce cereals.

Henry Wilson has a farm in the south west.
Here are some things he does in April. In what order do you think he does them? Put 1, 2, 3, etc. in each picture.

Listen. Henry Wilson is talking about his day. Write the time he says in each box in the pictures.

Was your order correct?

D He milks the cows and cleans the milking shed.

A He puts fertilizer on the fields.

B He has breakfast.

C He goes to bed.

H He checks the equipmen and does repairs.

G He eats lunch.

E He has dinner.

F He gets up.

I He takes his calves to market.

J He milks the cows.

Many people in Britain spend a lot of their free time in the country. There are 10 very big National Parks and people from the towns like to go there. Some people go walking or have a picnic. Other people do different sports.

Here are some of the things you can do in the National Parks. If you went on a holiday, what would you like to do?

I would like to …

Look at the map and find out where you can do different activities.

With your neighbour, write a letter to the British Tourist Authority to get more information.

Ask your teacher to send some of your letters to the British Tourist Authority in your country or in London. See what you receive!

your address
date

British Tourist Authority
Thames Tower
Black's Road
London W6 9EL
England

Dear Sir or Madam
Please can you send us some information about holidays in ...... We would like to....

Thank you.

Best wishes

your name

Collerosso
56010 Castel Maggiore
Pisa
ITALY
25th November

British Tourist Authority
Thames Tower
Black's Road
London W6 9EL
England

Dear Sir or Madam
Please can you send us some information about holidays in Scotland. We would like to go camping and canoeing next summer. Please can you also tell us about camping prices.

Thank you.

Best wishes

Piero Cunico

13 Revision and evaluation Units 9–12

1 Self-assessment How well do you know it?

How well do you think you know the
English you learned in Units 9–12?
Put a tick (✓) in the table for each thing.

Now choose some exercises to revise and
practise the things in the table.

	very well	OK	a little
Asking questions			
Numbers			
'my/his/her/their', etc.			
New words			

2 Present simple questions What's the question?

A   Here are some questions about elephants. Join them to the right answers.

a   They've got big ears, thick skin, and a long trunk.

1   How long does an elephant live?

b   In Africa and India.

c   For about sixty years.

2   What do they eat?

3   What do they look like?

d   Fruit, leaves and grass.

e   About four hours.

4   Where do they live?

5   How many hours do they sleep?

B   Look at the picture. Praying mantids are very strange creatures.
What questions can you ask about them?

Where … ?   What … ?   How … ?   Do …?

C   Now read about praying mantids. How many of your questions can you answer?

PRAYING MANTIDS are a type of insect.
They live in many parts of the world, including
the rainforests of South America and the
deserts of Africa. They eat small insects and
spiders but some big mantids eat small frogs
and birds. Some mantids eat other mantids.
They start with the head first so that they
cannot get away.

Mantids come in many different colours. Some
of them are very beautiful. The flower mantids
from Africa look like flowers. Insects land on
them to get food but, instead, the mantids eat
them! Mantids live for about five to seven years.

3 Numbers What's the number?

A Write the numbers in words.

41 *forty-one*   88 ....

97 ....   19 ....

32 ....   90 ....

20 twenty		**70** seventy
30 thirty		**80** eighty
40 forty		**90** ninety
50 fifty		**100** a hundred
60 sixty		**101** a hundred and one

B What's the answer?

forty-two + ten = *fifty-two*

twelve + twelve = ...

ninety – twenty = ...

sixty + thirty = ...

nineteen + eighty-one = ...

seventy – fifteen = ...

eighty-eight + thirteen = ...

thirty-five – seventeen = ...

ninety-seven – twenty-six = ...

4 Possessive adjectives This is my family

Fill in the missing words. Look back at your *Language Record* for help.

1 Hello. _ _ name's Tom.

2 This is _ _ sister. _ _ _ name's Sally.

3 And this is _ _ brother. _ _ _ name's Jack.

4 Here are _ _ parents. _ _ _ _ _ names are Peter and Susan.

5 This is _ _ fish. _ _ _ name is Jaws.

6 This is _ _ _ house.

7 What's _ _ _ _ name?

5 Vocabulary What's the word?

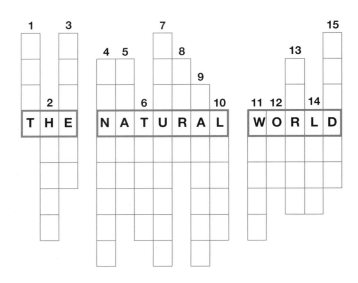

1 Lions eat ....

2 People sleep for about eight ....

3 An .... has got six legs.

4 An animal that lives in Australia.

5 Giraffes eat ....

6 Birds live in ....

7 A humming bird is a b............................. animal.

8 A parrot is a type of ....

9 Dolphins and whales are ....

10 Wild animals that live in Africa.

11 Fish live in ....

12 We are mammals. .... blood is warm.

13 Bats sleep .... the day.

14 How .... do cows live?

15 They eat bamboo.

6 Self assessment Were you right?

Look back at the chart in Exercise 1. Were you right?

7 How you learn Evaluation

7.1 Discussion Talk about your English work

First, with your class, decide which groups will look at Unit 9 or Unit 10 or Units 11 and 12.

Work in a group of three or four students. Decide who will report back to the class.
Look through your Units and, in your language, talk about these questions:

How well do you understand the Unit?
Did each Unit go too fast, just right, or too slowly?
Do you need to do some parts again?

Tell the rest of the class what your group said.

7.2 Your own ideas Easy or difficult?

What did you find easy in Units 9–12? What did you find difficult? Write down what you think.
Give your paper to your teacher at the end of the lesson. (You don't need to put your name on it.)

Theme C
The way we live

In Theme C you can learn
- to talk about food and your health
- to read and listen for specific information
- to use 'some' and 'any'
- to use object pronouns
- to talk about likes and dislikes
- to write a questionnaire
- to make your own test
- to think about how you are learning

Unit ☐

FIBRE cleans the inside of your body. There is fibre in nuts, beans and cereals.

minera...
vegetables,
meat, cereals a...
many other food...

DANGER!
HIGH IN CARBOHYDR...
HIGH IN SUGAR AN...
HIGH IN...
LO...

Unit ☐

Unit ☐

Unit ☐

All About YOU!

...ou get up?
...0 a.m. and 6.30 a.m.
...0 a.m. and 7.00 a.m.
...0 a.m. and 7.30 a.m.
...n.

...n meal?

Your inter...

4 **When do you w...**
a almost every...
b three or four...
c once or twice...
d almost neve...

What is your...
....

5 **Do you l...**
Yes ☐

Unit ☐

Take a look at Theme C

Where can you find the pictures?

Where can you find these things?
   something to make at home
   a game   a song

What is in the *Revision box* on page 77?

What can you learn in Unit 16?

14 Topic Food matters

1 Your ideas **The foods you like**

What is your favourite food?
Which foods don't you like?

Which foods do you think are good for you? Why?
Which foods do you think are bad for you? Why?

2 Reading **The food you eat**

Work by yourself. Write down your answers to the questions.
Compare answers with other students in your class.

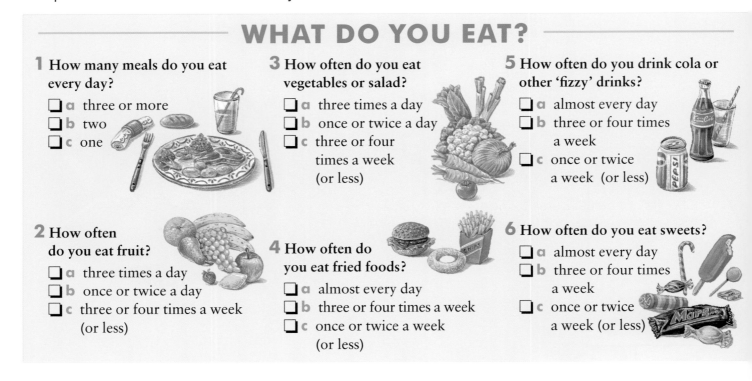

WHAT DO YOU EAT?

1 How many meals do you eat every day?
- ☐ a three or more
- ☐ b two
- ☐ c one

2 How often do you eat fruit?
- ☐ a three times a day
- ☐ b once or twice a day
- ☐ c three or four times a week (or less)

3 How often do you eat vegetables or salad?
- ☐ a three times a day
- ☐ b once or twice a day
- ☐ c three or four times a week (or less)

4 How often do you eat fried foods?
- ☐ a almost every day
- ☐ b three or four times a week
- ☐ c once or twice a week (or less)

5 How often do you drink cola or other 'fizzy' drinks?
- ☐ a almost every day
- ☐ b three or four times a week
- ☐ c once or twice a week (or less)

6 How often do you eat sweets?
- ☐ a almost every day
- ☐ b three or four times a week
- ☐ c once or twice a week (or less)

3 Vocabulary **How do you start the day?**

What do you have for breakfast? Tell your neighbour.

For breakfast, I have ...

some cereal

a croissant

an egg

some hot chocolate

some juice

some fruit

some bread

some rice

some milk

a pastry

4 Vocabulary Some more things to eat

Do you know the names of these foods? Label the pictures.

bread   butter
sugar   meat
fish   cheese
milk   vegetable
eggs   fruit
rice   pasta
potatoes

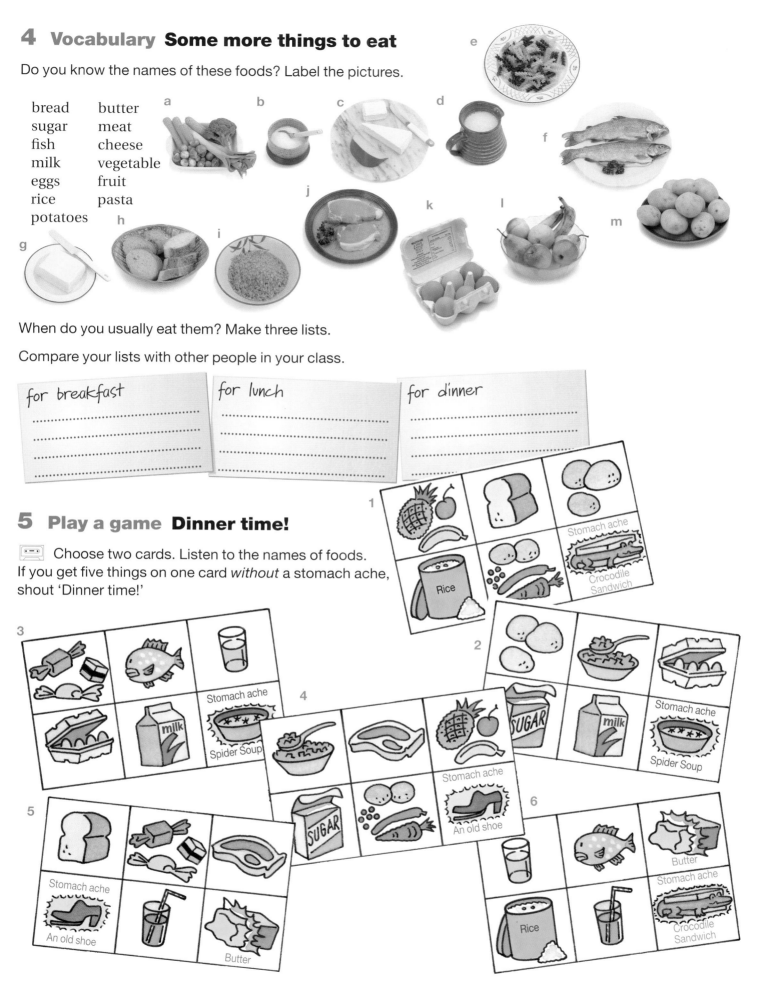

When do you usually eat them? Make three lists.

Compare your lists with other people in your class.

for breakfast	for lunch	for dinner
....	....	....
....	....	....
....	....	....
....	....	....

5 Play a game Dinner time!

Choose two cards. Listen to the names of foods.
If you get five things on one card *without* a stomach ache,
shout 'Dinner time!'

6 Reading Eat well, stay healthy!

Read about the foods we eat. Do *you* eat all of the 'seven important things'?

You can hear the article on the cassette.

EAT WELL *stay healthy*

Good food has seven important things.

CARBOHYDRATES give you energy. There are carbohydrates in bread, sugar, potatoes, pasta and rice.

FATS make you strong and give you energy. There are fats in meat, butter and cheese and oil.

VITAMINS are important for your eyes, your skin, your bones, your hair and for other parts of your body. There are 13 types of vitamins (A, B, C, and so on). There are vitamins in many types of food.

PROTEIN helps you to grow and gives you energy. There is protein in meat, fish and milk.

WATER is important for your blood. It also cleans your body from the inside. Drink lots of water every day!

MINERALS make your bones and teeth strong. There are different types of minerals in milk, vegetables, eggs, meat, cereals and many other foods.

FIBRE cleans the inside of your body. There is fibre in nuts, beans and cereals.

DANGER!
HIGH IN CARBOHYDRATES!
HIGH IN SUGAR AND SALT!
HIGH IN FATS!
LOW IN FIBRE!
LOW IN VITAMINS!

7 Reading In the supermarket

Read the text in Exercise 6 again and write the correct names on the signs.

VITAMINS IN ALL FOODS

carbohydrates

What is in these baskets? Carbohydrates, fats, fibre, protein, or minerals?

1   2   3   4

Which basket do you think is the best basket?

I think it is basket number … because it has some …   *It doesn't have any … in it.*

8   Decide …

You can work by yourself, with a partner or in a small group.
Choose **Exercise 8.1** or **Exercise 8.2**. Or you can do something else.
Talk to your teacher and decide. You can use the *Ideas list* on pages 150–151 to make an exercise.

8.1 Vocabulary   A puzzle

Can you complete the puzzle? What word do the clues spell?

Write a puzzle for other people in your class. Choose a long word and think of words to go across.
Write the clues and put the answers on the back. You can put it in your class *Exercise Box*.

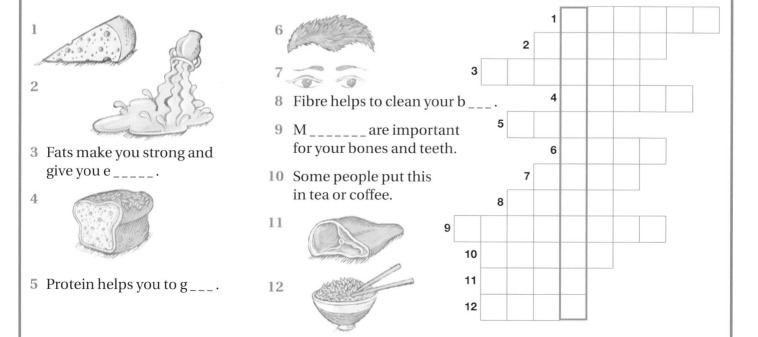

1

2

3 Fats make you strong and give you e _ _ _ _ _ .

4

5 Protein helps you to g _ _ _ .

6

7

8 Fibre helps to clean your b _ _ _ .

9 M _ _ _ _ _ _ are important for your bones and teeth.

10 Some people put this in tea or coffee.

11

12

8.2 Writing **Write a menu**

Read the article in Exercise 6 again. Write a healthy menu for a day that has all of the seven important things. Write a list for each meal.

9 Sing a song **I love chocolate**

Sing the song with your class.
The words are on page 155.

10 Review **Your Language Record**

Now complete your *Language Record*.

Time to spare? Choose one of these exercises.

1 Choose an exercise from your class *Exercise Box* or use the *Ideas list* on pages 150–151 to make an exercise for the *Exercise Box*.

2 Look at Exercise 7 again. Draw three more supermarket baskets:

   – one with a lot of carbohydrates and some fats
   – one with a lot of fibre and a lot of minerals
   – one with a lot of protein and a lot of fats

3 Choose three paragraphs from Exercise 6. Copy each sentence on to a small piece of paper. Mix them up. Can you put them in the correct order again? Give your exercise to another student to do.

Language Record

Write the meanings. Add the missing examples.

Word	Meaning	Example
a meal		How many meals do you eat a day?
a sweet		Do you want a sweet?
a vegetable		Do you like vegetables?
a body		Fats make your body strong.
bread		Bread has a lot of fibre in it.
butter		
sugar		Do you have sugar in tea or coffee?
meat		Do you eat meat?
breakfast		What time do you have breakfast?
lunch		
dinner		When do you have dinner?
important		
less		I eat sweets less than once a week.
often		How often do you eat fruit?
give		Carbohydrates give you energy.
make		Fats make you strong.
clean		
help		

Choose four more words. Write some examples and the meanings.

cheese   an egg   fruit   rice   pasta   a potato   oil   eyes   skin
bones   teeth   hair   healthy   different   milk   once   twice   three times

15 Language focus
'some' and 'any', pronouns

1 Your ideas **Can you cook?**

Do you like cooking? Do you know any recipes? Tell the class.

2 Listening **What are they making?**

Look at the recipes and listen.

Pat and Anne want to make something. What is it?
Can they make it? What *can* they make?

PANCAKES
You need:
2 cups of flour
1 cup of milk
1 cup of water
1 egg

SHORTBREAD BISCUITS
You need:
350g of flour
225g of butter
100g of sugar
some salt

PAT: OK. Let's see. What do we need?
        Have we got any flour?
ANNE: Yes. We've got lots of flour. Here.
PAT: Good. We need some butter, too.
        Have we got any butter?
ANNE: Some butter … butter …
        We've got a lot of milk, but butter …
        Ah, yes. Here we are.
PAT: Excellent.
ANNE: We've got six eggs. Do you want them?
PAT: Er … no. We don't need any eggs. Sugar?
ANNE: Sugar … sugar … sugar. No!
        We haven't got any sugar.
PAT: Oh no! I know! We can make …

3 Grammar **What have we got?**

3.1 Your ideas **What do you say?**

How do you say these sentences in your language?

   We've got some eggs.   We haven't got any butter.   Have you got any sugar?

What do 'some' and 'any' mean in your language?

3.2 'some' and 'any' **A grammar puzzle**

When do you say 'some'? When do you say 'any'?
Read the example sentences. With your neighbour, work out a rule.

You say 'some' when …   You say 'any' when …

Compare your rule with other students. Then compare it with the rule that your teacher has.

Have we got any flour?
Have we got any butter?
Do we need any eggs?

We don't need any eggs.
We haven't got any sugar.
I haven't got any money.

We need some butter.
For breakfast, I have some bread and milk.
We've got some eggs.

3.3 Practice **with 'some' and 'any'**

First label the things in this picture.

   bread   cheese   butter   eggs
   sugar   fish   potatoes   milk

Now, test your memory. Look at
the picture for a few moments.
Try to remember what is in it.
Then close your book.

Your teacher will say the names
of some foods. Write a sentence about each one. For example:

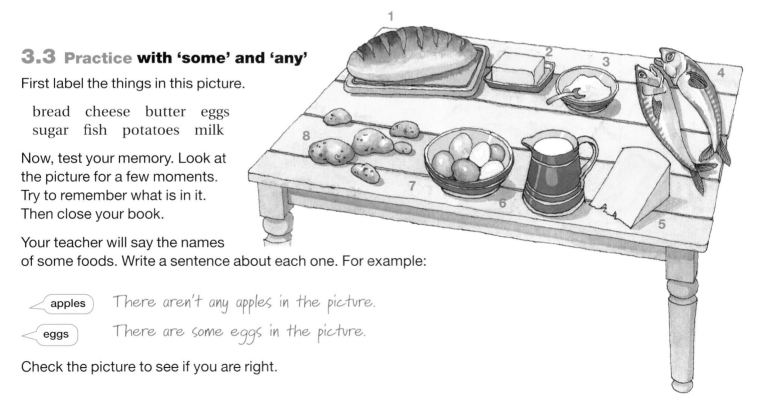

apples   There aren't any apples in the picture.

eggs   There are some eggs in the picture.

Check the picture to see if you are right.

4 Grammar 'them, it, her, him' ...

4.1 Your ideas What do you say?

How do you say these sentences in your language?

Vitamins are important. You need them!   That's Peter. Do you know him?
This is my new bike. Do you like it? There's Sujita. Can you see her?

Words like 'them', 'it', 'him' and 'her' are called *object pronouns*. Draw a line to show what each one talks about.

Vitamins are important. You need them!

4.2 Practice What do you like?

Work with your neighbour. Ask each other about the pictures.

Do you like ...?

I	like don't mind hate	it. him. her. them.

I think	it's he's she's they're	nice. beautiful. OK. interesting. boring. horrible.

Tarzan

THE WORLD

Geography

milk

cats

football

cola

spiders

fish

vegetables

Maths

dogs

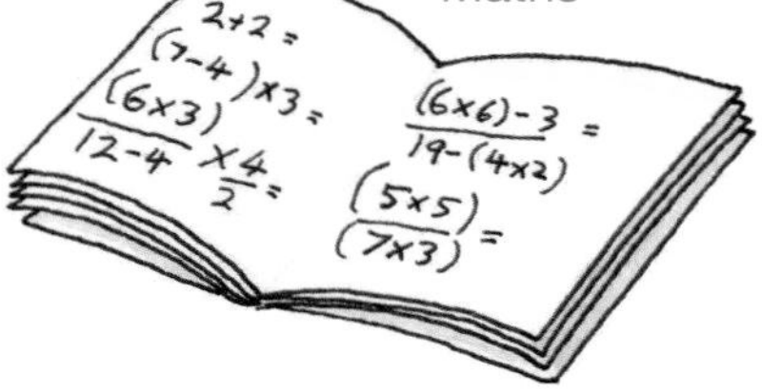

sweets

spaghetti

Out and about with English

5 Language functions Likes and dislikes

5.1 Your ideas Sophie visits Mona's house

Sophie is in Mona's house. Look at the picture.
What do you think they are talking about?

5.2 Listening Are you right?

Listen. Are you right? Do you like Mona's music?

MONA: Well. This is my bedroom.
SOPHIE: Oh … er, it's very nice.
MONA: No, it's not! It's terrible!

SOPHIE: Well, yes …
MONA: But I like it. I've got a new CD. The
          Mash Boys. Do you like them?
SOPHIE: The Mash Boys. I don't know them.
MONA: What! Listen. What do you think?
SOPHIE: Well, it's not my favourite music. I like
          Sleeping Giants.
MONA: Oh, yeah. They're nice. Here. Listen to
          this. Do you like it?

SOPHIE: Pardon?
MONA: Do you like it?
SOPHIE: Well it's OK.
MONA: Pardon?
SOPHIE: No, I don't like it.
MONA: Oh, OK.

5.3 Practice Do you like it?

Now you try it. Work with a partner.
Talk about your friend's things.
You can change Mona and Sophie's dialogue.

Act out your dialogue for the class.

Do you like it/them?
I think it's/they're nice   terrible   beautiful
interesting   boring   horrible …

Have you got any …?

This is my …

house

bedroom

pet cat

pet dog

pet rabbit …

These are my …

games

books

cars

dolls …

Something to make at home

IMPORTANT!
Do this with an adult

You can make pancakes and shortbread at home.

Pancakes

You need:

2 cups of flour   1 cup of water
1 cup of milk   1 egg

① Mix everything together.

② Put some of the liquid into a frying pan.

③ Cook the pancakes on both sides.

④ Delicious with lemon and sugar!

Shortbread biscuits

You need:

350g of flour   100g of sugar
225g of butter   some salt

① Mix everything together.

② Put into a cooking tin.

③ Put it into the oven at 170°C for one hour.

④ Cut it into pieces. Delicious with a glass of milk!

6   Review **Your Language Record**

Now complete your *Language Record*.

Time to spare?   Choose one of these exercises.

1 Choose an exercise from your class *Exercise Box* or use the *Ideas list* on pages 150–151 to make an exercise for the *Exercise Box*.

2 Match the parts of the words with the pictures.

br
but
chee
e
mil
po
su

ter
tatoes
se
k
ggs
gar
ead

3 Write three sentences that are true and three sentences that are false about your house or bedroom. Ask another student to guess which sentences are false.

There are three bedrooms in my house. True!
There aren't any televisions in my house. False!

c ....

d ....

e ....

4 Reading At home with the Greens

The Green family live in a small, terraced house. Their house is more than 100 years old. They have a small garden at the back of their house. Upstairs, there is the bathroom and three bedrooms. Downstairs, there is the kitchen, a living room and a room where the television is.

Here is a plan of their house. Put the pieces in the correct places.

Are houses in your country like the Sharmas' house or the Greens' house? How are they different from houses in your country?

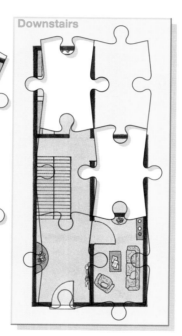

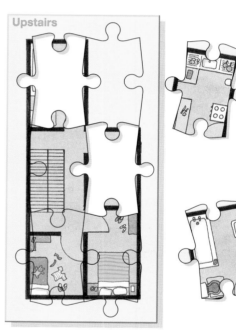

5 Listening In the living room

Here is a picture of a living room in England. Can you label each part?

a wall   a bookcase
curtains   a carpet
a sofa   a fire   a table
a chair   a lamp   a vase

What do you have in your living room? Tell the class.

📟 Mrs Green is talking about her living room. What is in it?

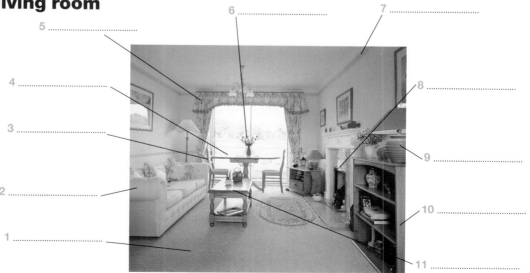

18 Revision and evaluation Units 14–17

1 Self-assessment **How well do you know it?**

How well do you think you know the
English you learned in Units 14–17?
Put a tick (✓) in the box.

	very well	OK	a little
Say what you think about something			
New words (about food)			
'some' and 'any'			
'me/you/him/her/us/them'			

2 An example test **Test yourself**

Work with your neighbour and do this short test.

When you have finished, check your answers on page 84.
Then look at Exercise 1 again. Were you right?

TEST YOURSELF

A Likes and dislikes **Say what you think**

Write your answers.

1 What do you think of football?
I .... it.
I think it's ....

2 Do you like cats?

3 What do you think of Maths?

4 Do you like snakes?

5 Do you like this boat?

6 What do you think of this woman?

B Vocabulary **Food**

What's the word?

1 Breakfast, lunch and dinner are ....

2  ....

3 Bananas and apples are ....

4 .... comes from cows.

5 ....

C Grammar **'some' and 'any'**

What's on the table?
Write some sentences, like this:

bread – cheese

There is some bread and some cheese.
sugar – eggs

There is some sugar but there aren't any eggs.

1 milk – salt
2 cheese – fish
3 butter – sugar
4 water – flour

....
....
....
....

....
....
....
....

D Grammar **'me/you/him/her/us/them'**

Fill in the gaps.

1 This is my brother.
Do you know ....?

2 This is my sister.
Do you know ....?

3 These are my pictures.
Do you like ....?

4 This is my new bag.
Do you like ....?

5 It's very heavy.
Can you help ....?

3 Do it yourself! **Write your own test**

Work in small groups. Look back at Units 14–17 and write part of a test for your class.
Look at the test in Exercise 2 for ideas. Tell your teacher which part you are doing.

   A Say what you think   **B** New words   **C** 'some' and 'any'   **D** 'me/you/him/her/us/them'

Give the test to your teacher to check and to put together for your class.

4 How you learn **Evaluation**

4.1 Discussion **Talk about your English work**

First, with your class, decide which groups will look at Unit 14 or Unit 15 or Units 16 and 17.

Work in a group of three or four students. Decide who will report back to the class.
Look through the Units you chose and talk about these questions:

Unit 14 groups:
  Was the topic interesting?
  Do you want to learn more about food?
  What was the best part in the Unit for you? Why?

Unit 15 groups:
  Was the grammar in the Unit clear?
  Do you need more practice?
  What was the best part in the Unit for you? Why?

Units 16 and 17 groups:
  Was it easy to make the questionnaire?
  How can you work better next time?
  What did you learn in Unit 17?

Tell the rest of the class what your group said.

4.2 Your own ideas **Future lessons**

Do you need more practice with anything? What do you want to do in future lessons?
Write down your ideas. Give your paper to your teacher.
(You don't need to put your name on it.)

Answers to the test in Exercise 2

A Say what you think
Example answers: 1 I like it. I think it's exciting.   2 Yes, I like them. I think
they're nice.   3 I don't mind it. I think it's OK.   4 No, I hate them. I think
they're horrible.   5 I don't mind her.   6 I don't mind her. I think
she's OK.

B New words
1 meals   2 some cheese   3 fruit   4 Milk   5 an egg

C 'some' and 'any'
1 There is some milk and some salt.
2 There is some cheese but there isn't any fish.
3 There is some butter and some sugar.
4 There isn't any water or any flour.

D 'me/you/him/her/us/them'
1 him   2 her   3 them   4 it   5 me

Theme D
Planet Earth

Unit ☐

In Theme D you can learn
- to talk about space, the stars and the planets
- the Present continuous
- comparatives and superlatives
- how to ask for travel information
- to write poems
- listen and read specific information
- how to make your own test
- to think about how you are learning

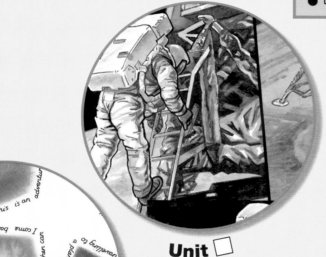

Unit ☐

TEST YOURSELF!

Unit ☐

Unit ☐

Unit ☐

Take a look at Theme D

Where can you find the pictures?

Where can you find these things?
- a listening exercise
- a reading exercise
- a writing exercise
- a speaking exercise

What can you do with a balloon on page 90?

19 Topic Into space

1 Your ideas The planets

🔲 Listen to part of Holst's *The Planets Suite.*
While you are listening, look at the pictures in this Unit.

Do you like the music? What things do you imagine when you hear it?
What do other students in your class think?

2 Reading Our place in space

Look at the pictures again and read about space.
While you are reading, make some notes.
Like this:

> Things I knew already
>   The Earth is 75% water.
> Things I didn't know
>   The sky is history.
> Things I don't understand
>   expand?
>   gravity?

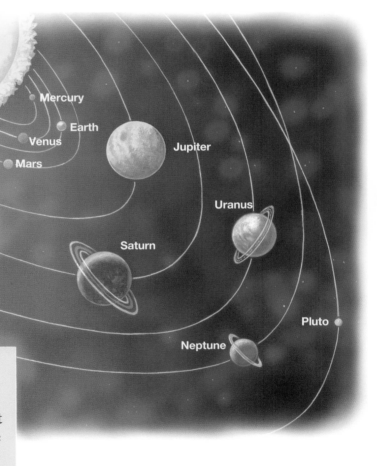

When you are ready, compare your notes with your
neighbour. Help each other to understand the text.

1 OUR SOLAR SYSTEM

There are nine planets in our solar system. The
smallest planet is Pluto. It is also the coldest because it
is a long way from the sun. The Earth goes around the
sun in $365\frac{1}{4}$ days (one year) but Pluto takes 248 years!

2 THE UNIVERSE IS EXPANDING!

Astronomers know that the universe is expanding.
The stars are moving away from each other. They are
not sure why this is happening. Our sun is a star, too.
We are moving with the sun.

Language Record

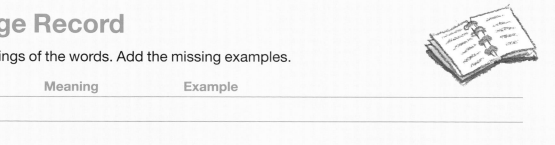

Write the meanings of the words. Add the missing examples.

Word	Meaning	Example
a neighbour		
a picture		
a ship		
alone		Are you alone?
light (adj.)		On the moon, you are much lighter.
light (n.)		The sun gives us light.
same		
so		I don't have any money so I can't go to the film.
strong		The gravity on Earth is stronger than on the moon.
weak		Gravity on the moon is very weak.
sure		I'm not sure.
collect		He's collecting rocks.
expand		The universe is expanding.
go down		He's going down the ladder.
happen		What is happening?
leave		The spaceship is leaving.
move		
pull		Pull the door to open it.
put		He's putting his foot on the moon.
take		Can I take a sweet?
take		It takes many years for light to come from the stars.

Choose four more words. Write some examples and the meanings.

gravity   air   life   perhaps   a star   size   nearer   the tide

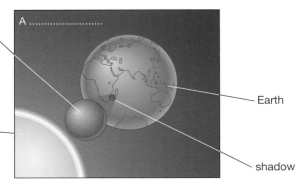

moon

sun

Earth

shadow

A ....

1 Reading **Night in the day**

Are you afraid of the dark? Sometimes it is dark during the day …

Read the texts. Which diagram shows an eclipse of the sun? Which diagram shows the eclipse of the sun and which shows the eclipse of the moon? Label the diagrams.

> If the moon goes between the Earth and the sun, we have an *eclipse of the sun*. The moon stops the light from the sun and we have night in the day.
>
> If the Earth goes between the moon and the sun, we have an *eclipse of the moon*. The moon goes into the shadow and it disappears for a few minutes.

Have you ever seen an eclipse?

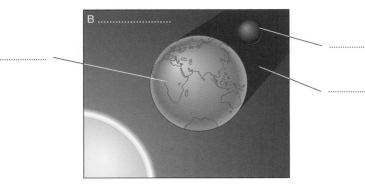

B ....

2 Listening **Mexico, 1992**

In 1992 in Yucatán, Mexico, there was a very clear eclipse. Listen to what the American television presenter said at the time.

Is she talking about an eclipse of the sun or an eclipse of the moon? Can you write the correct time for numbers 1–7 under the picture?

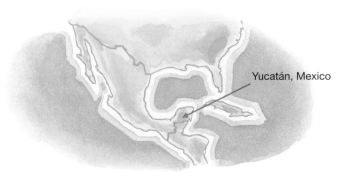

Yucatán, Mexico

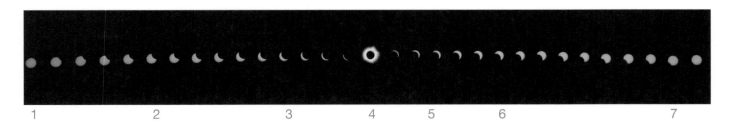

1   2   3   4   5   6   7

Language Record

Asking for travel information Write the meanings.

Which bus goes to …? ....

What time does the bus go? ....

What time does the bus come back? ....

How much is the ticket? ....

Single .... Return ....

The Present continuous Complete the tables. Add some more examples.

I'm (I'm not)
You are (aren't)
He ....
She ....
It ....
They ....
You ....

reading a book.
writing a letter.
making a drink.
singing a song.

Am
Are
....
....
....
....
....

I
you
he
she
it
they
you

coming?
speaking clearly?
sitting in your chair?

Comparatives and superlatives Complete the table.

adjective	big	high	....	....	....	bad
comparative	bigger	....	taller	....	better	....
superlative	the biggest	....	....	the longest	....	....

Revision box Prepositions

1 Prepositions tell us where something is. Fill in the missing word.

The monkey is … the box.   *next to*

2 Prepositions also tell you when something happens. Fill in the missing words.

I go to school …

3 Play Preposition Bingo!
Complete the sentence. Choose one word for each gap.

I can meet you
… the clock tower
under   behind
next to   in front of

… o'clock
at 9   at 11
at 10   at 12

on the first …
Wednesday
Thursday

Friday
Saturday

in …
June
July

August
September

If your teacher says your place, time, day or month, put a tick (✓).
The first person to meet your teacher is the winner.

21 Activity
Poems from the Earth and space

Step 1 The words in your head

Think about the stars, planets, and space and write down the words and phrases you can remember. You can listen to the cassette while you think. It has some more of Holst's *The Planets Suite*.

Pluto

The sun is very hot

SPACE

The sky is history

The moon

stars

Step 2 Talk to your neighbour

Show your words to your neighbour and look back at Unit 19. Do you want to add any words? Talk to your neighbour about what your words mean.

Step 3 Imagine ...

You are travelling in space. You can see the Earth from your rocket. What more can you see? What can you hear? Is it nice in space or horrible? Is it exciting?

Imagine that the Earth can speak. What does it say? Is it happy? Is it sad? What does it like? What does it want? What does it think? Tell the rest of the class your ideas.

Step 4 Write a poem

Write a poem about your ideas. You can imagine that you are travelling from the Earth or you can imagine that the Earth speaks. Read your poem and make changes as you write.

Listen to some examples.

I am old.
I am very old.
Millions of people live on me.
I give them food.
I give them air.
I give them life.

I can see the stars in the sky.
Millions of stars.
The moon looks at me.
The sun shines.
I can see space.
Space, space, space.
Lots of space!

For more ideas, show your poem to your neighbour
and look back at Unit 19.
You can write your poem in a shape.

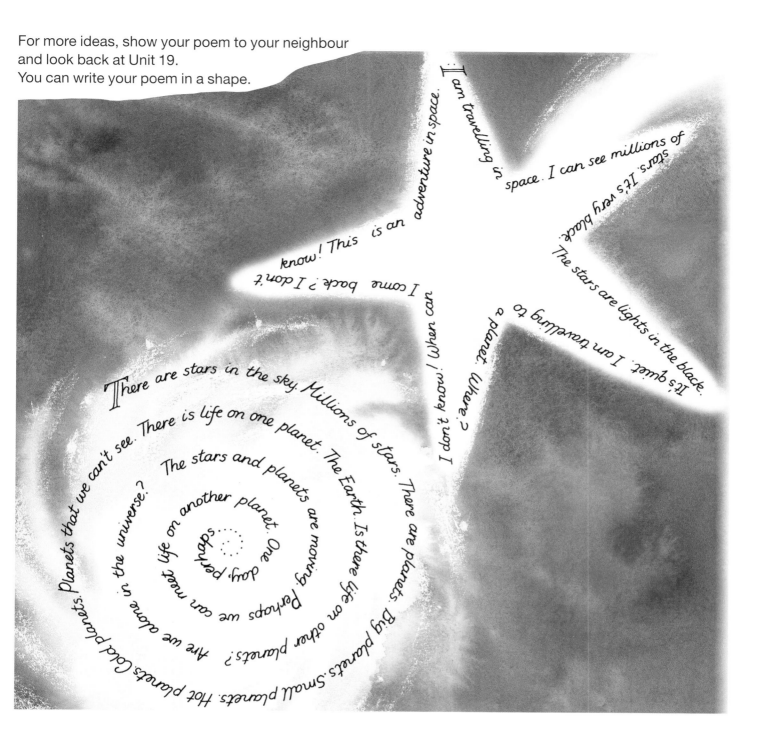

The poem, written in a star and spiral shape:

I am travelling in space. I can see millions of stars. It's very black. The stars are lights in the black. It's quiet. I am travelling to a planet. Where? I don't know! When can I come back? I don't know! This is an adventure in space. I...

There are stars in the sky. Millions of stars. There are planets. Big planets. Small planets. Hot planets. Cold planets. Planets that we can't see. There is life on one planet. The Earth. Is there life on other planets? Are we alone in the universe? The stars and planets are moving. Perhaps we can meet life on another planet. One day, perhaps...

Step 5 **Show each other your poems**

Either put your poems on the wall and walk around the class to read the other poems
or sit in a small group and read your poem to the other students.
Which parts do you like from the other students' poems?

Step 6 **How you learn: evaluation**

Discuss these questions with the people in your class.

Was it easy or difficult to write the poems? Did you like writing poems?
Would you like to do it again? How? Alone? In a group? In your book? On a poster?

22 Culture matters
Life by the sea

1 Your ideas **About your country**

Is the sea important in your country's history? How? Is it important today? How?

Do you live near the sea? Look at the pictures in this Unit. Does the sea look like this in your country?

2 Reading **Britain and the sea**

The sea is very important in Britain. There are many towns and ports on the coast. There are also many holiday places by the sea. Fishing and shipbuilding were once very important in Britain's history. Today, the sea is still important. A lot of Britain's oil and gas comes from the sea.

Look at the pictures. Does your country have the same type of places?

Listen. Write the correct number under each picture.

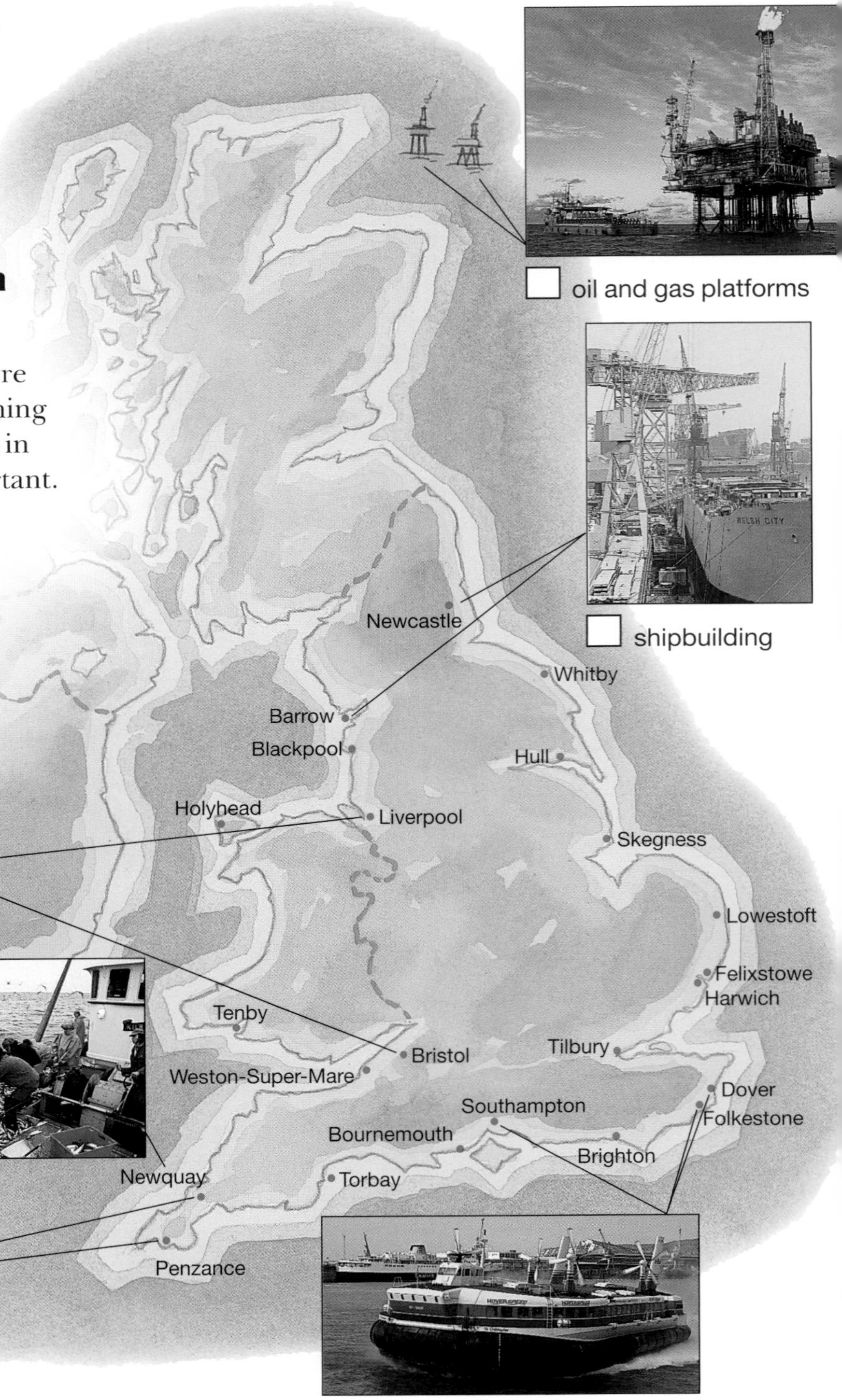

oil and gas platforms

shipbuilding

Newcastle
Whitby
Barrow
Blackpool
Hull
Holyhead
Liverpool
Skegness
Lowestoft
Felixstowe
Harwich
Tenby
Bristol
Tilbury
Weston-Super-Mare
Dover
Folkestone
Southampton
Bournemouth
Brighton
Newquay
Torbay
Penzance

important ports

fishing

beaches

boats and hovercraft to other countries

3 Reading **The moon, the sun and the sea in Britain**

Read about the tides in Britain. Can you find three good things about the tides and three bad things?

There are many countries that do not have tides. Does your country have them?

Sometimes the tides are very high and this can be a big problem for towns near the coast. These towns have very high walls to stop the sea. London has a special mechanical 'wall' to stop the tide coming into the city.

The Thames Barrier, London

There are big differences between 'high tide' and 'low tide' in Britain. In some places, the sea goes out a very long way. In the summer, for example, you can walk from England to Wales! As the tide comes in and goes out, it cleans the beaches. In the ports, the ships wait for the high tide. At low tide, it is impossible to go in or out of the port.

Low tide, Weston-Super-Mare

The tides can also help to make electricity. There are plans to make electricity in the sea near Bristol.

Cardiff
Bristol
Weston-Super-Mare

Britain is disappearing! In the winter, the very strong winds and the high tides 'eat' parts of Britain. In some parts of Britain, the sea is 'eating' almost six metres of coast each year.

A hotel in England falls into the sea

4 Your ideas
Fun at the seaside

There are many things to do at the seaside. Can you label the pictures? Choose the correct words.

play games on the beach
go windsurfing lie on the sand
go diving go water-skiing
go fishing go swimming

Imagine that you can go to the seaside for a day. What would you like to do? Tell the class.

I'd like to …

~ COME TO THE SEASIDE! ~
Look at all the things you can do!

You can …

go windsurfing

1 Self-assessment How much do you know?

How well do you think you know the English you learned in Units 19–22?
Put a tick (✓) in the box.

	very well	OK	a little
Say what is happening now (Present continuous)			
Compare things ('big, bigger, the biggest', etc.)			
Ask for travel information			
New words			

2 An example test Test yourself

Work with your neighbour and do this short test.

When you have finished, check your answers on page 104. Then look at Exercise 1 again. Were you right?

TEST YOURSELF

A Present continuous What is he saying?

Write a sentence for each picture.

B Comparatives **Fill the gap**

Sunshine 1930   Moonshine 1950

1 Sunshine is .... than Moonshine.

2 She is .... than him.

3 His nose is .... than her nose.

4 Bengo is .... than Rex.

C Language functions **Ask for travel information**

What are these people saying? Write their conversation.

Can you tell me which bus goes to Oldtown?

Number 34

Bus number: 34

Bus from the school to Oldtown: 9.30

Price: single £ 1

D Vocabulary **New words**

Put the letters in the correct order. Match the words with the pictures.

1 ONOM   2 NLEPAT   3 LULP   4 NEPO   5 RTONGS

MOON

3 Do it yourself! Write your own test

Work in small groups. Look back at Units 19–22 and write part of a test for your class.
Look at the test in Exercise 2 for ideas. Tell your teacher which part you are doing.

A Say what is happening.   **B** Compare things.   **C** Ask for travel information.   **D** New words.

Give the test to your teacher to check and to put together for your class.

4 How you learn Evaluation

4.1 Discussion Talk about your English work

First, with your class, decide which groups will look at Unit 19 or Unit 20 or Units 21 and 22.

Work in a group of three or four students. Decide who will report back to the class.
Look through the Units you chose and talk about these questions:

Unit 19 groups:	Unit 20 groups:
Was the topic interesting?	Was the grammar in the Unit clear?
Do you want to learn more about space?	Do you need more practice?
What was the best part in the Unit for you? Why?	What was the best part in the Unit for you? Why?

Units 21 and 22 groups:
  Did you like writing poems?
  Do you want to try again?
  What did you learn in Unit 22?

Tell the rest of the class what your group said.

4.2 Your own ideas What do you think?

Write down what you think. Give your paper to your teacher at the end of the lesson.

Answers to the test in Exercise 2

A What is he saying?
2 She's playing football.
3 He's cooking.
4 They're playing with the computer.
5 I'm talking to you!

B Comparatives
1 Sunshine is more expensive than Moonshine.
2 She is taller than him.
3 His nose is longer than her nose.
4 Bengo is happier than Rex.

C Ask for travel information
Man: Can you tell me which bus goes to Oldtown?
Woman: Number 34.
Man: What time is the bus in the morning?
Woman: It goes at half past nine.
Man: How much is a single ticket?
Woman: It's £1.
Woman: Thank you. Goodbye.
Man: Goodbye.

D New words
1 Moon 2 planet 3 pull 4 open 5 strong

This is Australia
is very dry in Australia.
u don't have much rain. They
a lot of hot weather. In
l August they

Unit ☐

Theme E
Natural forces

In Theme E you can learn

● to talk about the weather
● frequency adverbs
● countables and uncountables
● more comparatives and superlatives
● to use the Present continuous to talk about future plans
● to write about the world's weather
● to read and listen for specific information
● to think about how you are learning

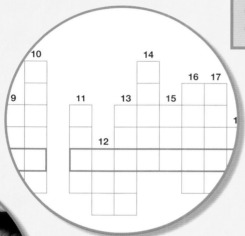

Unit ☐

Unit ☐

Unit ☐

Unit ☐

Take a look at Theme E

Where can you find the pictures?

Where can you find these things?
  some music by Beethoven
  something to do with a balloon at home
  a song

What is in the Revision box on page 117?

24 Topic The weather

hot weather

1 Your ideas Musical weather

🔲 Listen to the cassette. You can hear part of Beethoven's 6th Symphony, about the weather. Do you like the music? Why/Why not?

Which of the pictures describes the music best?

What type of weather do you like? Look at the pictures again and tell the class.

I like warm weather.
I don't like …
I don't mind …

strong winds

warm weather

snow

thunder and lightning

cold weather

rain

2 Frequency adverbs
What's the weather like in your country?

Look at the calendar. What weather do you have in your country? Copy the calendar and make some notes.

rain
warm weather
hot weather
cold weather
snow
strong winds
thunder and lightning

Tell the rest of the class your ideas.

strong winds and rain

January	February	March	April
May	June	July	August
September	October	November	December

We	always
	usually have … in …
	sometimes
	never

3 Frequency adverbs **We never have snow in June!**

Work in pairs. Look at the calendar again. Write six sentences about your weather. Make some true and some untrue.

Give your sentences to another pair. They have to correct the untrue sentences.

1. We always have snow in June.   *Not true! We never have snow in June.*
2. We sometimes have rain in July and August.   *True!*
3. It is colder in June than February.   *Not true! It is colder in February.*

4 Listening **What's the weather like?**

Look at the pictures. When do you have weather like that in your country? What type of day is today?

Listen to the people on the cassette. What type of day are they talking about?

a windy day

a sunny day

a rainy day

a chilly day

a foggy day

a cloudy day

5 Sing a song **Singing in the rain**

Sing the song with your class. The words are on page 155.

6 Reading **Where does the weather come from?**

Why do we have rain? Why are there winds? Tell the class what you think. Are these sentences true or false?

1 Hot air rises.

2 Cold air rises.

3 We have winds because trees move.

4 High up in the sky, it is very hot.

5 Clouds are water vapour.

7 Reading **Why do we have rain?**

Work in pairs. Put the sentences in the correct place.

The cold cloud meets a warm cloud.
The water becomes water vapour.
The wind blows the clouds.

Compare answers with other students.

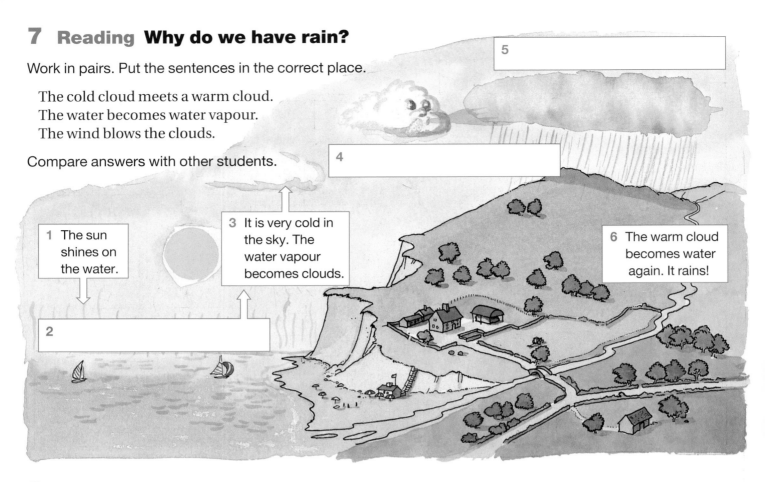

5

4

1 The sun shines on the water.

3 It is very cold in the sky. The water vapour becomes clouds.

6 The warm cloud becomes water again. It rains!

2

8 Reading **Why do we have winds?**

Work in pairs again. Put the sentences in the correct place.

The wind blows.
The ground becomes warm.
The air rises.

Listen and check your answers.

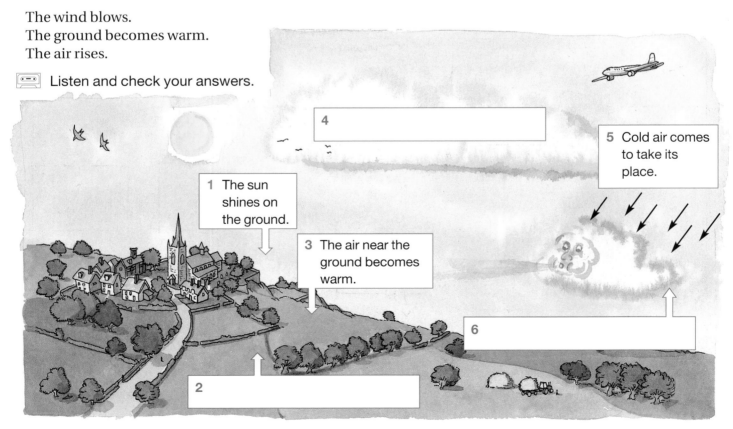

4

5 Cold air comes to take its place.

1 The sun shines on the ground.

3 The air near the ground becomes warm.

6

2

9 Decide ...

You can work by yourself, with a partner or in a small group.
Choose **Exercise 9.1** or **Exercise 9.2**. Or you can do something else.
Talk to your teacher and decide.
You can use the *Ideas list* on pages 150–151 to make an exercise.

9.1 Vocabulary **What's the word?**

Join the word halves together and then match them to the meaning.
Write the complete word.

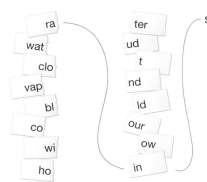

 something from the clouds = *rain*

= ....

not hot = ...

something in the sky = ...

= ....

 = ...

 = ...

 = ...

Now look at Exercises 1–8 and make another word exercise. (You can also put the meanings in your language.) Give your exercise to some other students to do or put it in the *Exercise Box*.

9.2 Reading **Why do we have lightning?**

Can you put in the missing words? Draw the missing picture.

cloud   rises   colder   falls   expands   make   jumps

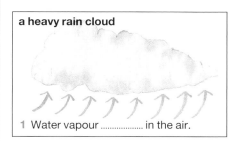

a heavy rain cloud

1 Water vapour .... in the air.

2 Inside the cloud, the water vapour becomes .... It becomes ice.

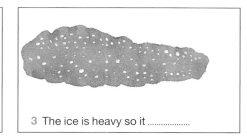

3 The ice is heavy so it ....

4 More water vapour is rising inside the cloud but the ice is falling. When they meet, they .... static electricity.

BANG!

5 The static electricity .... to the ground and makes lightning.

The lightning warms the air. The air .... very fast and makes a bang!

Three experiments to try at home!

IMPORTANT! Do this with an adult

A Make your own cloud

1. Fill a plastic bottle with hot water. Leave it for five minutes.
2. Pour $\frac{3}{4}$ of the water away.
3. Put some ice on the top of the bottle.
4. Wait and watch! In a few minutes, there is a cloud.

B Hot air rises ...

1.
2. Put the bottle in a bucket of hot water. The air rises into the balloon.

C ... and cold air falls

1. Warm the bottle in hot water.
2. Put a balloon on the bottle.
3. Put the bottle in cold water.

10 Review **Your Language Record**

Now complete your *Language Record*.

Time to spare? Choose one of the exercises.

1. Choose an exercise from your class *Exercise Box* or use the *Ideas list* on pages 150–151 to make an exercise for the *Exercise Box*.

2. Are these sentences true about your country? Write 'True' or 'Not true' and correct the sentence.
   1. We often have snow in August.
   2. It is warmer in February than in December.
   3. It is windier in November than in June.
   4. We never have sunny days in April.
   5. It is sunnier today than yesterday.
   6. We also have rain in November.

3. Look at the calendar in Exercise 2. Write a sentence about what you do in each month. For example:

   In June, we often go to the beach.

Language Record

Write the meanings. Add the missing examples.

Word	Meaning	Example
a cloud		Rain comes from clouds.
the sky		Look at the clouds in the sky.
the sun		The sun is very hot today.
the wind		Why do we have winds?
weather		Do you like hot weather?
snow		Do they have snow in Sweden?
thunder and lightning		Do you like thunder and lightning?
always		We always have rain in April.
never		We never have snow in June.
usually		
sometimes		
to blow		The wind blows the leaves from the trees.
to meet		What time can we meet?
to not mind		I don't mind cold weather.
to rise		
to shine		The sun shines on the plants.
cold		It's never very cold in my town.
warm		It isn't very warm in England.
hot		The sun makes the ground hot.
strong		We have strong winds in June.
sunny		
fast		

Choose three more words. Write some examples and the meanings.

| windy | chilly | rainy | wonderful | to warm | to become ice | water vapour | foggy |

25 Language focus
Uncountables, comparing

1 Reading **The midnight sun**

The countries at the North and South Poles have very short days in winter and very long days in summer. They have sun at midnight! The sun goes down and then rises again.

Look at the map on page 153. Which countries are near the North Pole?

2 Speaking **Near the North Pole**

Look at the information about June and December in a country near the North Pole – Norway. Are June and December like that in your country?

Work in pairs. Ask each other questions, like this:

How many sunny days do they have in December?
How many rainy days do they have in June?
How many windy days do they have in December?

Compare your answers with other students in the class.

> **Remember!**
> There are *four* weeks in a month!

Now calculate the answers to these questions:

1 How much rain do they have in December?
2 How much rain do they have in June?

3 How much sun do they have in December?
4 How much sun do they have in June?

WEATHER IN NORWAY

One week in June

	Mon	Tue	Wed	Thur	Fri	Sat	Sun
Hours of sunlight	20	20	20	20.5	20.5	20	20
Rain/snow in mm	0	0	0	0	0	0	0
Wind (kph)	5	10	5	8	0	0	5

One week in December

	Mon	Tue	Wed	Thur	Fri	Sat	Sun
Hours of sunlight	3	3	4	3	3.5	3.5	3
Rain/snow in mm	150	0	0	0	30	0	0
Wind (kph)	40	25	25	30	40	45	15

3 Grammar 'How many rainy days ...?' and 'How much rain ...?'

3.1 Your ideas A grammar puzzle

When do you say 'much'? When do you say 'many'? Look at these
sentences and try to make a rule. Talk about it with your neighbour.

How many rainy days are there in June?
We don't have many sunny days in March.
We have many windy days in December.

How much rain do you have May?
We don't have much sun in April.
We don't have much water in the summer.

3.2 Countables and uncountables Can you count?

In English, you can count some things but not others. For example, you
can say 'five days' but you can't say 'five rain'. Work with your neighbour.
Write 'C' (countable) or 'U' (uncountable) by each word.

water   sunny days   clouds   snow   hours of sunshine   rain   windy days   ice

Do you use 'much' with countables or uncountables? What about 'many'?
Say a sentence for each word:

We don't have much/many ...   *Do you have much/many ... ?*

3.3 Summary Questions, negative sentences and positive sentences

We use 'much' and 'many' with questions
and negative sentences. We use 'a lot of',
'lots' and 'many' with positive sentences.

? and –	+
much	a lot of
many	lots
	many

3.4 Practice What are they saying?

Work with your neighbour. What is each person saying?
Write a sentence for each of these things. For example:

We have a lot of sunny days here.   *We don't have much water.*

Compare your answers
with other students.

[cassette] Check your
answers with
the cassette.

rain

snow

windy days

water

clouds

sunshine

sunshine

foggy days

water

4 Grammar It's sunnier and more beautiful than yesterday

4.1 Adjectives with 'y' Sunnier, windier …

Do you remember how to make comparisons with short adjectives?
Complete these sentences:

A year on Earth is … a year on Mercury.
A year on Pluto is …

Kilimanjaro is … K2.
Mount Everest is …

Most adjectives are like 'long' and 'high', but some are different! Adjectives with 'y'
change to '-ier' and '-iest'. Like this:

A: It's a sunny day today.
B: Yes, it's sunnier than yesterday.
A: I think it's the sunniest day of the year!

Work in pairs. Practise the following words in the same way.

windy   cloudy   rainy   foggy

What about your weather now? Is it sunnier than yesterday? Is it colder than yesterday?

4.2 Long adjectives It's more modern!

Long adjectives don't use '-er' and '-est'. With long adjectives,
you have to say 'more' and 'the most'. Like this:

A: Which one do you like: this car or that one?
B: That one.
A: Why?
B: It's more modern!

With your neighbour, practise with these adjectives.

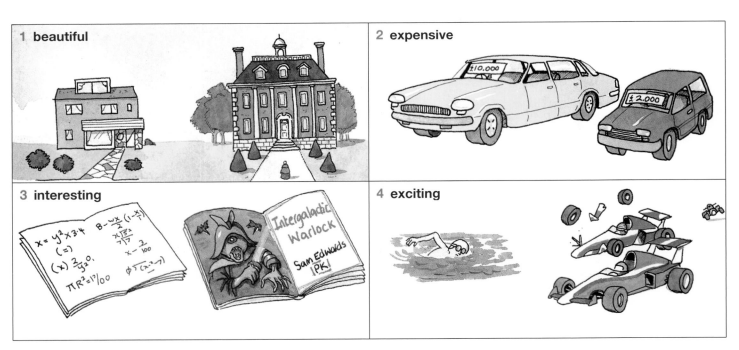

1 beautiful

2 expensive

3 interesting

4 exciting

Out and about with English

5 Language functions Making plans

5.1 Your ideas It's Sophie's birthday

It's Sophie's birthday on Sunday. She wants to have a party on
Sunday afternoon. She telephones Mona to ask her if she can come.
What do you think she says?

5.2 Listening Can you come?

Listen to Sophie on the telephone.
Does she say what you think?

Why can't Mona come on Sunday?
Why can't she come on Saturday?
What is Barbara doing on Friday?

MONA:	Hello.
SOPHIE:	Hi, Mona! It's Sophie.
MONA:	Hi, Sophie. What are you doing?
SOPHIE:	Well, I'm planning my birthday party. I want to have a party on Sunday afternoon. Can you come?
MONA:	Oh. I'm going to my grandmother's on Sunday.
SOPHIE:	Oh no. What about Saturday?
MONA:	Saturday. On Saturday, I'm playing tennis.
SOPHIE:	Oh no. When are you free?
MONA:	Well, Friday is fine.
SOPHIE:	OK. We can have the party then. Can you tell Ali?
MONA:	Of course.
SOPHIE:	Good. See you at school. Bye.
MONA:	Bye.

Sophie rings Barbara:

BARBARA:	Hello.
SOPHIE:	Hi, Barbara! It's Sophie.
BARBARA:	Hi, Sophie.
SOPHIE:	Barbara, are you free on Friday? After school.
BARBARA:	No, I'm not. I'm going to the dentist.
SOPHIE:	Oh, that's OK. What time?
BARBARA:	Four o'clock.
SOPHIE:	Can you come to my house after the dentist? I'm having a party.
BARBARA:	Great! Yes.
SOPHIE:	OK. Good. See you tomorrow. Bye.
BARBARA:	Bye.

5.3 Practice **Your week**

Now you try it. Work with a partner. You want to meet your friend. But when?
Write down what you are doing on five days.

> going to the dentist   playing …   going swimming   doing my homework
> going to …   going shopping with …   helping …

YOUR WEEK		YOUR FRIEND'S WEEK
Monday		Monday
Tuesday		Tuesday
Wednesday		Wednesday
Thursday		Thursday
Friday		Friday
Saturday		Saturday
Sunday		Sunday

Now ask your partner. Find out when he/she is free. (Don't look!) Write down
his/her answers. Take turns to ask.

> *Are you free on …?   No, I'm not.   On … I'm -ing …*
> *What are you doing on …?   On …, I'm -ing …*

When can you meet? Act out your dialogue for the class.

6 Review **Your Language Record**

Now complete your *Language Record*.

> # Time to spare? Choose one of these exercises.
>
> 1 Choose an exercise from your class *Exercise Box* or use the *Ideas list* on pages
>   150–151 to make an exercise for the *Exercise Box*.
>
> 2 Write about the months of the year in your country.
>   Use these words: hot   cold   windy   dry   wet   sunny
>   For example: *June is the wettest month.   December is the sunniest month.*
>
> 3 Look back in your book. Write your answers to five of these questions:
>
> | Unit 3: | Where does David live? |
> |---|---|
> | Unit 4: | What does Mona want for her mother? |
> | Unit 9: | How long do cows sleep? |
> | Unit 10: | Where does Sophie live? |
> | Unit 14: | Why are fats good for you? |
> | Unit 15: | Do you need eggs for shortbread? |
> | Unit 19: | How far away is the moon? |
> | Unit 20: | When is the next solar eclipse? |
> | Unit 24: | What does hot air do? |
> | Unit 25: | What countries have the Midnight Sun? |

Language Record

Making plans

Write the meanings.

Can you come on Saturday?	....
Are you free on Sunday?	....
What are you doing on Monday?	....
What about Tuesday?	....
On Wednesday, I'm going to my friend's house.	....
Thursday is fine	....

Some countables

snakes, cows, clouds ....

Some uncountables

air, milk, rain ....

'much' and 'many' in questions

How much rain falls in Mexico?

'much' and 'many' in negatives

There aren't many people here.

'a lot of' and 'lots' in positive sentences

I've got a lot of brothers and sisters.

Long adjectives

Complete the table.

Adjective	Comparative	Superlative
exciting	more exciting	the most exciting
interesting	....	....
	more beautiful	....
sunny	sunnier	....
windy	....	....

Revision box The Present simple

1 Look at these pictures.

Write:
  what three of them do
  what three of them don't do
  a question about three of them

(You can look at Units 3, 9, 14, 19 and 24 for help.)

For example:
Elephants eat leaves.
People don't lay eggs.
Where does rain come from?

2 Have a quiz!

Work in a small group. Write down five questions about Units 3, 9, 14, 19 and 24. Give your questions to your teacher. Mix them up. See which group can answer five questions correctly!

26 Activity
A poster: weather around the worl

Before your lesson

Step 1 Copy the map

Copy a world map onto a big piece of paper.

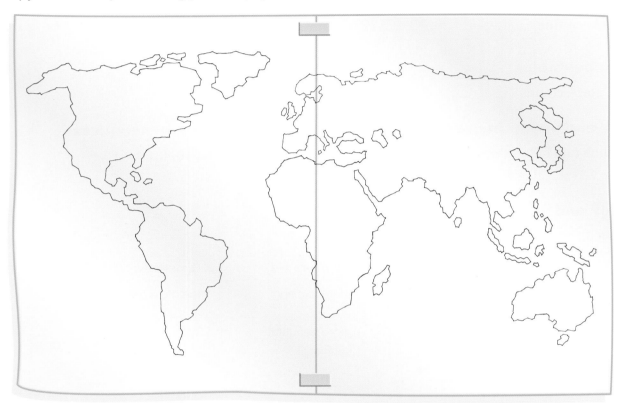

Step 2 Collect some information

Talk to your family and friends. Ask them about the weather in different parts of the world.

Where do they have a lot of rain?
Where don't they have much rain?

Do they have hot weather in Australia?
Do they usually have cold weather in England.

Ask about a lot of countries!

In your lesson

Step 3 Tell everybody your information

What is the weather like in different parts of the world?
Tell the class your ideas and what you found out.

Step 4 Make a poster

Work in a small group or with a partner. Draw lines to places on your map.
Write about the weather there.

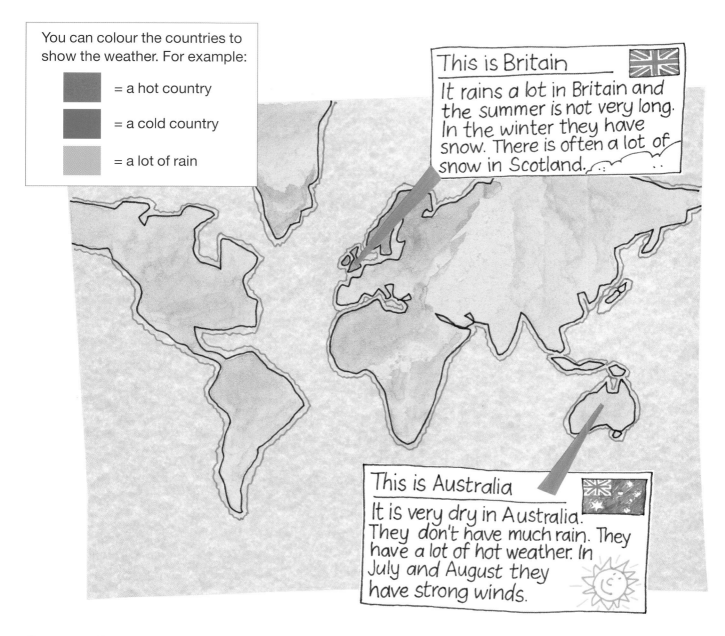

You can colour the countries to
show the weather. For example:

■ = a hot country

■ = a cold country

■ = a lot of rain

This is Britain

It rains a lot in Britain and
the summer is not very long.
In the winter they have
snow. There is often a lot of
snow in Scotland.

This is Australia

It is very dry in Australia.
They don't have much rain. They
have a lot of hot weather. In
July and August they
have strong winds.

Step 5 Show your maps to each other

Show your map to other students in the class or put them on the wall.
Read and talk about what you have done.
Do you have the same information for the countries?

Step 6 How you learn: evaluation

Discuss these questions with people in your class.

Was it easy or difficult to write about the weather?
Is it easier or more difficult to write with another person?
If you did it again, what would you do differently?

27 Culture matters
Living with nature

1 Your ideas Seasons in your country

Which of these seasons do you have in your country?

spring   summer   autumn   winter

When are they? Are they very different?
What different things do people do in each season?

When is your favourite time of the year? Why?

2 Reading The seasons in Britain

The four seasons in Britain are very different. Read about
what Daniel and Fiona think about autumn and winter.

Some phrases are missing. Can you choose the correct ones?

> we have a lot of snow   it is already dark
> The leaves on the trees go brown
> we have to wear warm clothes

Check your answers with the rest of
the class.

Winter Poem by Fiona
December, January, February.

Christmas trees in the windows.
Central heating's on.
The days are shorter now.

Autumn Poem by Daniel
September, October, November.

Scarves, hat, jumper, gloves.
Fantastic fun, kicking leaves.
Animals hibernate.

Winter
It's very cold in winter!
Sometimes, ... and we can make snowmen.
I don't like winter because we can't go out very much.
We have to wear thick clothes and, in our house, we
have the heating on all the time. When we come home
from school at 4 o'clock, ... Horrible! But
there is one good thing about winter – Christmas!

Autumn
Autumn is a very
beautiful time of the year.
.... and then
they fall off. We play
outside a lot but
....
School starts again in
Autumn, at the
beginning of September.
At school, we have conker
competitions.

3 Reading Spring and summer

Now read what Daniel and Fiona think about spring and summer.
Which of the four seasons is their favourite?
Which season don't they like?

Spring Poem   by Daniel
March, April, May.
A long winter sleep.
   Birds singing in the trees.
   Flowers opening.

Spring

After the long winter, spring is great!
There are new leaves on the trees and
the birds start to sing. We can go outside
again and play in the park. The days are
longer and it doesn't get dark until about
six o'clock. It's much warmer but it rains
a lot and the days are very windy.

Summer Poem by Fiona
June, July, August.
Running in the park.
   Voices laughing, happy.
   Yellow sun, blue skies.

Summer

Summer is the time for me! School
finishes in July and we can play outside
all the time. Sometimes (but not often!) it
is very hot. People are happier and they
talk to each other a lot more. The days
are very long. In June, for example, it
doesn't get dark until about 10 o'clock.
It's very difficult to go to sleep at night!

You can listen to Daniel and Fiona on the cassette.

What games do you think the children are playing in
each picture?

Choose one of the texts and read it again.
How is that season different in your country?
Make some notes and then tell the class what you think.

4 Two games In the park

Here are two games that children in
England like to play. Try them out now
and play them with your friends later!

CONKERS

Put a piece of
string through
a conker
(a horse chestnut
or any hard nut).

Try to hit your
friend's conker.
The first conker
to break loses!

HOPSCOTCH

Draw this on the ground. Play with
some friends and take turns to go.

Throw a stone to 1. Don't step on 1.
Hop to 2–3, hop to 4, put two feet
on 5–6, hop to 7, put two feet on
8–9 and hop to 10. Turn round and
do the same to go back to 1. On your
next turn, throw the stone to 2 and
go up to 10 and back again.

Miss a turn if you: drop the stone;
miss the number with your stone;
put your feet on the lines or fall over.

The first person to throw the stone
to 10 and hop up and back is the
winner!

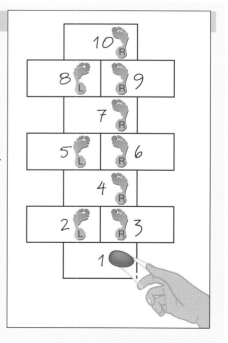

28 Revision and evaluation
Units 24–27

1 Self-assessment How much do you know?

How well do you think you know the
English you learned in Units 24–27.
Put a tick (✓) in the box.

Now choose some exercises to revise
and practise the things in the table.

	very well	OK	a little
Say how often you do something ('often, sometimes, usually', etc.)			
Compare things			
Use 'much' and 'many'			
New words			
Make plans			

2 Frequency adverbs I never do that!

Write your answers to these questions. Use these words:

sometimes   never   always   usually

For example: *I never get up before seven o'clock.*

1 Do you ever get up before seven o'clock?
....

2 Do you ever have breakfast in bed?
....

3 Do you ever go to bed after midnight?
....

4 Do you ever speak English at home?
....

5 Do you ever eat sweets?
....

6 Do you ever drink cola?
....

Compare your answers with other students in your class.

3 Comparing It's bigger and better

Write about the cameras. Use the words.

Snappy

DX500

1 The DX500 *is bigger than the Snappy.*

2 The DX500 .... (modern)

3 .... (heavy)

4 .... (new)

5 .... (difficult to use)

6 .... (small)

7 .... (light)

8 .... (expensive)

4 Countables, uncountables 'How many ...?' or 'How much ...?'

Are these words countable or uncountable? Make two lists.

eggs milk giraffes air food trees water cars lions clouds
water vapour snow meat wind blood leaves people

Now fill the gaps with 'much', 'many' or 'a lot of'.

1 How .... lions
are there in the zoo?

2 There is .... water
vapour in that cloud.

3 Do you eat ....
meat?

4 There aren't ....
trees in the Sahara.

5 How .... cars are
there in your town?

6 Giraffes eat .... leaves.

7 How .... rain
falls in Brazil?

8 There aren't ....
people here.

5 Vocabulary What's the word?

Write the words in the puzzle.
What three words
do they spell?

1 Clouds are _ _ _ _ _ vapour.
2 The sun _ _ _ _ _ _ .
3 An important star near us.

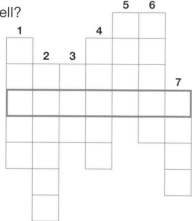

4 It's a very _ _ _ _ _ day.

5 _ _ _ _ air falls.
6 Hot air _ _ _ _ _ .
7 _ _ _ _ comes from clouds.
8 The month before June.
9 The month before July.
10 They are white and in the sky.
11 The month after June.
12 Very, very cold water.
13 The sun gives us heat and l _ _ _ _ .'
14 The month after February.

15 The sun is very h _ _ .

16 It's a very s _ _ _ _ day.
17 The month after March.
18 It's white and cold and it comes
from the clouds.
19 The month before September.

6 Making plans **What are you doing next week?**

Write down what you are doing on Monday to Saturday next week. Write your own ideas or choose from the list.

going to the dentist   playing …
going swimming
doing my homework   going to …
going shopping with …   helping …

YOUR WEEK	
Monday	
Tuesday	
Wednesday	
Thursday	
Friday	
Saturday	
Sunday	*Free*

Now write your answers to Nina's questions.

NINA: Hello. Are you free on Monday?

YOU: ....

NINA: What about Tuesday? What are you doing on Tuesday?

YOU: ....

NINA: Wednesday is not possible for me. I'm going to the dentist's. What are you doing?

YOU: ....

NINA: Thursday is difficult.

YOU: ....

NINA: On Friday I'm going to my grandmother's and on Saturday I'm going shopping with my mother. What about Sunday?

YOU: ....

NINA: You're free on Sunday! Excellent! Do you want to do my Maths homework for me on Sunday?

YOU: ....

NINA: You don't want to! Oh no! OK, I can ask Susan. Goodbye!

YOU: ....

7 How you learn **Evaluation**

7.1 Discussion **Talk about your English work**

First, with your class, decide which groups will look at Unit 24 or Unit 25 or Unit 26 and 27.

Work in a group of three or four students. Decide who will report back to the class. Look through the Unit you chose and, in your language, talk about these questions.

What did you find easy in the Unit?   Where do you think you need more practice?
Did it go too fast / just right / too slow?   What suggestions do you have for things to do in class?
What did you find difficult?

7.2 Your own ideas **What do you think?**

Write down what you think. Give your paper to your teacher at the end of the lesson.

Theme F
Living history

Unit ☐

Unit ☐

Unit ☐

AIR MAIL

Andrew Littlejohn and Diana Hicks
c/o Cambridge University Press
ELT Group
The Edinburgh Building
Shaftesbury Road
Cambridge CB2 2RU
England

Unit ☐

In Theme F you can learn
- to talk about life in the past
- to use 'was' and 'were'
- Past simple
- read and listen for specific information
- to talk about past events
- to write about your family and friends
- to write your own test
- to think about how you learn

Unit ☐

Take a look at Theme F

Where can you find the pictures?

Where can you find these things?
  a listening exercise
  a reading exercise
  a writing exercise
  a speaking exercise

What can you do in Unit 31?

29 Topic
The cavepeople

1 Your ideas 15,000 years ago

15,000 years ago, people lived in caves. Look at the picture. How was life for cavepeople?

exciting   boring   horrible
nice   dangerous   safe
hard   easy   difficult
happy   unhappy

Tell the class your ideas.

I think life was exciting.
I think cavepeople were happy.

Say it clearly!
was /wəz/
were /wə/

2 Listening In a cave

🔊 Listen. What can you hear? Make a list.

I can hear …

Compare your list with other students. Do you think the cave is a nice place? Is it dry or wet? Is it cold?

3 Reading A dangerous life for cavepeople!

3.1 Writing

Life was very dangerous for cavepeople. Why? Brainstorm your ideas with your neighbour.

It was very cold in winter — A dangerous life for cave people

3.2 Reading

How many dangers can you find in the text? Add them to your ideas map.

 You can listen to the text on the cassette.

Nogoba – the cavegirl

Nogoba was a cavegirl. She lived in a cave with about 40 other people. Cavepeople lived in big groups to help each other. Their lives were very dangerous. There were many wild animals near the caves – lions, tigers, bears and elephants.

The cavemen hunted. They killed the animals for food.

The children's jobs were dangerous, too. Nogoba and her friends went to the river every day to get water. Sometimes, the river was very deep. Sometimes, there were animals near the river.

For many months of the year, Nogoba was cold. There was ice and snow everywhere. It was difficult to be warm. The children sometimes went to sleep by the fire. Sometimes they were too near the fire.

Sometimes Nogoba and her friends went to find fruit and nuts to eat. Sometimes the fruit and nuts were poisonous and everyone became ill. There weren't any cave doctors or cave hospitals!

4 Speaking **A dangerous life today**

There are many dangers in modern life.
Brainstorm your ideas with the class.

5 Writing **'Differences' poster**

How is life different today?
Make a 'Differences' poster.

Put your poster on the wall.

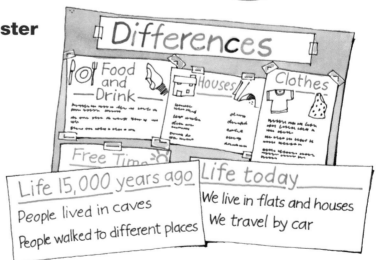

6 Sing a song **Caveman Rock**

📼 Sing the song with your class.
The words are on page 155.

7 Reading **Cavepeople painted and hunted**

Work with a partner. Read one text each.

How many questions can you answer from the text?

1 How did they make paint?
2 How did the cavepeople kill animals?
3 What did they put on their bodies? Why?
4 What animals did they hunt?
5 Where did they paint the pictures?

6 What part of the animal did they eat first?
7 Where did they keep their paint?
8 Why did they paint animals upside down?
9 When did they paint pictures?
10 What did they use for clothes?

📼 You can listen to the texts on the cassette.

Hunting and cavepeople

Cavepeople hunted together in a big group. They hunted mammoths, tigers and bears. They put animal fat on their bodies. The fat helped to keep them warm and it was difficult for the animals to hold them. They also used the animal fat for lights. In the night, they made terrible sounds and the animals were frightened. The animals went into a river or sometimes they went over a big cliff. The cavepeople killed the animals with spears. They liked to eat the soft meat first (the heart and the brains) and then they cooked the body of the animal. They used the skins to make clothes.

Cave paintings

There are cave paintings in caves in many different countries. Cavepeople painted pictures of the animals that they hunted. Cavepeople hunted mammoths, tigers and bears. They painted the pictures inside their cave. Sometimes the cavepeople painted the animals upside down to show that the animals were dead. They made their paint from different plants to make green, yellow and brown. They kept their paint in animal bones. They painted their pictures before and after a big hunt.

8 Decide ...

You can work by yourself, with a partner or in a small group.
Choose **Exercise 8.1** or **Exercise 8.2**. Or you can do something else.
Talk to your teacher and decide.
You can use the *Ideas list* on Pages 150–155 to make an exercise.

8.1 Speaking A game: Danger!

Play in a group of four. You need a dice and four counters. See the rules on page 149.

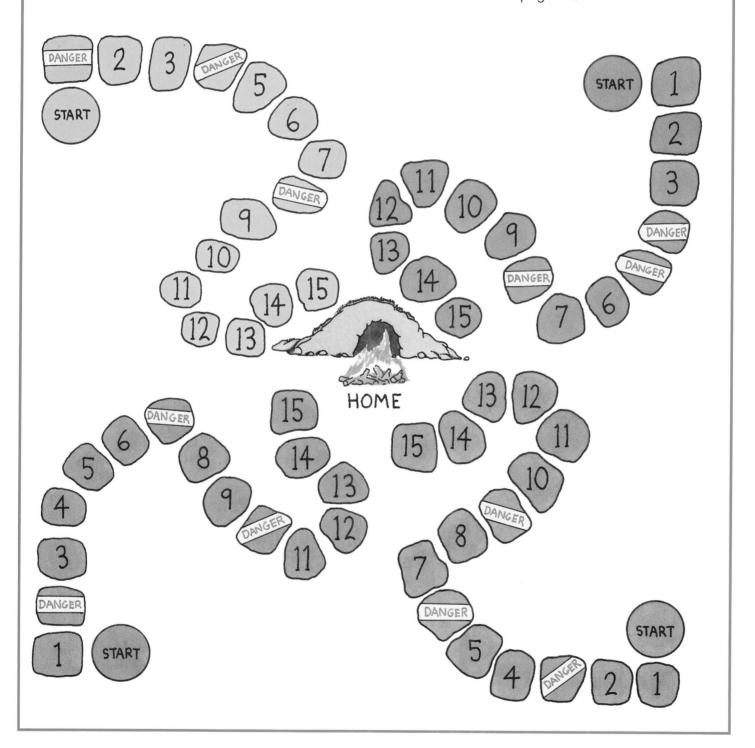

8.2 Reading **What changed first?**

When did the life of cavepeople change?
Match the sentences a–e with the numbers 1–5
on the timeline.

a They painted pictures on the walls of the caves.
They had pots for water and food.

b They picked fruit and killed animals for food.
They moved to a different place every night.

c They lived in small houses.
They had sheep and goats.
They had wool for clothes.

d They lived in caves. They
had stone tools and skin
bags for their tools.

e They lived in villages.
They were farmers and had
fruit and vegetables for food.

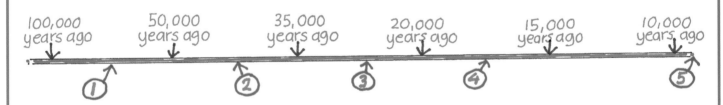

100,000 years ago   50,000 years ago   35,000 years ago   20,000 years ago   15,000 years ago   10,000 years ago

① ② ③ ④ ⑤

Now match the inventions to this timeline. Add some more inventions.

People had cars.   People used telephones.   People used electricity.   People used computers.
People went to the moon.   People went by train.   People went to school.

1850   1870   1890   1910   1930   1950   1970   1990

9 Writing **'Differences' poster**

Can you add some more ideas to your 'Differences' poster?

10 Review **Your Language Record**

Now complete your *Language Record*.

Language Record

Write the meanings. Add the missing examples.

Word	Meaning	Example
a cave		
a picture		
fat		
skin		The cavepeople used animal skin to make clothes.
dangerous		
dark		It is very dark inside the caves.
deep		It is dangerous to swim in deep water.
exciting		It was exciting to hunt an animal.
frightened		The animals were frightened of the sounds.
happy		
upside down		Cavepeople painted animals upside down.
wild		
chase		The hunters chased the animals into the river.
hunt		
kill		They killed animals with spears.
paint		
pick		The children picked nuts and fruit to eat.
went		The animals went into the river.

Choose some more words. Write some examples and the meanings.

poisonous   safe   ice   soft   attack   a cliff   a goat   a spear   a sheep

Time to spare? Choose one of these exercises.

1 Choose an exercise from the *Exercise Box* or use the *Ideas list* on pages 150–151 to make an exercise.

2 Are these sentences true [T] or false [F]? Write some more true/false sentences.
    a Cave people were vegetarians. ☐   **c** They liked paintings. ☐
    b They cooked their food. ☐   **d** They had telephones. ☐

3 Imagine you are a caveperson. Draw a picture and write about your life.

30 Language focus
Past simple

1 Your ideas Your first day at school

Tell the class what you can remember.

What was the name of your first school?
Was it big or small?
Can you remember your first classroom?
How many children were there?
Who was your teacher?
How old were you?

My first school was …
It was a small/big school.
The classrooms were …
There were …
My teacher's name was …
I was … years old.

2 🎞 Listening Sophie's first day

Barbara is asking Sophie about her first school.
Listen and answer the questions.

What was Sophie's first school?   Was it big or small?
What was her classroom like?   How old was she?

Was your first school bigger than Sophie's?   Was it newer?
Were you older than Sophie?

BARBARA:	Sophie, where did you go to school before?
SOPHIE:	I went to a school in Scotland.
BARBARA:	Was it nice?
SOPHIE:	Yes, it was a very small school. It had 86 pupils.
BARBARA:	That's very small!
SOPHIE:	Yes, but there were a lot of children in each classroom. There were 32 in my classroom. There were only three classrooms.
BARBARA:	Was it an old school?
SOPHIE:	Yes, it was very old. It was more than 200 years old. We were in the best classroom. In the other rooms, in the winter, there was ice inside the rooms!
BARBARA:	Oh! When did you start school?
SOPHIE:	At nine o'clock.
BARBARA:	No, I mean, how old were you?
SOPHIE:	About four and half.
BARBARA:	Oh. I was five, I think …

3 Grammar **Were you older? Was it newer?**

3.1 Your ideas **'was' and 'were'**

When do you say 'was' and 'were'? Look at these
sentences from Units 29 and 30 and complete the tables.

I was four years old.
It was exciting.
It was dangerous.
Cavepeople were farmers.
She was a cavegirl.

We were in the best classroom.
There was snow everywhere.
There were many wild animals.
How old were you?
The river was very deep.

I	....	older.
You	....	happy.
He		12 years old.
She	....	very cold.
It		
We	....	
They	....	

There	....	only three classrooms.
There	....	ice in the classroom.

3.2 Practice **Was it cold?**

Choose the best question to continue each conversation.

a I went swimming on Saturday.
b I went to the cinema at the weekend.
c I went to bed at 6 o'clock last night.
d I went in a helicopter yesterday.
e We walked home last night.
f My mother helped me with my homework yesterday.
g I cooked a meal yesterday.

1 Was it a long way?
2 Were you excited?
3 Was the film good?
4 Were you tired?
5 Was it difficult?
6 Was the water cold?
7 Was it good?

3.3 Practice **Spot the differences**

How many differences can you find
between the morning and the afternoon?
Write a sentence about each one.

In the morning there was ... There were ...

In the afternoon

In the morning

4 Grammar Some more Past tense verbs

4.1 Your ideas What do you say?

In your language, do many verbs in the Past tense look the same? Are some verbs very different?

4.2 Past tense form What's the difference?

Find the verbs in Lists A and B. How are the verbs different?

LIST A

We walked home last night.
My mother helped me with my homework yesterday.
I had a lot of homework last night.
I saw Peter yesterday.
I went to bed at 6 o'clock last night.
I made a cake yesterday.

LIST B

I walk home every night.
She always helps me with my homework.
I always have a lot on Monday night.
I usually see him on Thursday.
I usually go to bed at 9 o'clock.
I usually make a cake on Sunday.

4.3 Practice Past verbs

In English, you add '-ed' to the end of many verbs to make the Past tense.
Complete the text with Past tense of the verbs.

THE LIFE OF THE CAVEPEOPLE

Cavepeople .... (live) more than 30,000 years ago. They
.... (walk) from place to place and they .... (use) stones
to make tools. They .... (hunt) in big groups and ....
(kill) animals for their food. They .... (cook) the meat on a
fire in front of their cave. Often, they .... (paint) pictures of
the animals in their caves.

Other verbs are very different. Look at List A in 4.2 and complete these sentences.

CAVE MUSIC

Sometimes, the cavepeople .... (make) music with bones from
animals. They .... (have) many pipes to blow and many things to
bang. They .... (play) with their fingers. They .... (use) the
pipes to tell each other about dangerous animals. They also ....
(use) the pipes when they .... (go) hunting. If they .... (see) an
animal, they .... (make) a lot of noise.

🎞 Listen and check your answers.

4.4 Some more practice What did you do?

Ask your neighbour.

What did you do on
Monday ... Tuesday ...?

I saw ....

I played ....

I went to ....

Out and about with English

5 Language functions **Talking about the past**

5.1 Your ideas **It was fun!**

Tell the class about somewhere you went where you had fun.

Last weekend … Last month … Last summer …
I went to … I saw … I made … I had … I played … I was …

They can ask you questions.

Was it nice? Where was it? Was it exciting? Was it big?
Were you frightened? Were you with your friends?

5.2 Your ideas **Sophie's party**

Sophie and Mona are at a party.
Look at the picture. What do
you think they are saying?

5.3 Listening **Are you right?**

 Listen to Sophie and Mona.

S: Do you like the party?
M: Er … yes. I think so. I went to a different type of party last week.
S: Was there any music?
M: Yes. But it was different. There was a sitar.
S: What's that?
M: Like a big guitar … and a tabla …
S: What's that?
M: A special type of drum.
S: Was it a dancing party?
M: No, not really. Do you like dancing parties?
S: Yes! I went to a party last week, too.

M: Was it like this?
S: No. It was great. It was a swimming party.
M: A swimming party?!
S: Yes. We had races and games in the swimming pool.
M: Was it a birthday party?
S: Yes.
M: Was there a birthday cake?
S: Yes, but it went in the water!

5.4 Practice **What did you do?**

Now you try it. Work with a partner. Talk about something you did. Here are some ideas:

Last weekend …   Last month …   Last summer …
I went to …   I saw …   I made …   I had …   I played …   I was …

You can ask your partner some questions.

Was it noisy?   Was it quiet?   Was there music?   Was there dancing?
Were your friends there?   Was it a birthday party?   Was the food nice?

Act out your dialogue for the class.

6 Review **Your Language Record**

Now complete your *Language Record*.

Time to spare? Choose one of these exercises.

1 Choose an exercise from your class *Exercise Box* or use the *Ideas list* on pages 150–151 to make an exercise for the *Exercise Box*.

2 Write the Past tense of the verbs in the sentences. Write an exercise for other students.
   a I .... in Japan for five years. (live)
   b She .... the car on Sunday. (clean)
   c He .... his hair last night. (wash)
   d We .... at the party for three hours. (stay)
   e The children .... television last night. (watch)

3 What is the first thing you can remember?
   The thing I can remember is when I was … years old.
   I went/saw/made/visited/played …

Language Record

Talking about past events Add more phrases. Write the meanings.

What did you do last night? ....

I went to ....

I saw ....

I made ....

I had ....

I played ....

What was it like? ....

It was great. ....

'was' and 'were' Complete the table and add some more examples.

I	was	
You	....	
He	....	here yesterday.
She	....	very cold last night.
It	....	happy at school.
We	....	
They	....	

There were ....

There was ....

....

....

....

Past tense regular verbs

Complete the sentences.

Cavepeople .... from place to place. (walk)

They .... animals. (hunt)

They .... meat on a fire. (cook)

They .... in caves. (live)

They .... music together. (play)

Past tense irregular verbs

Complete the sentences.

Cavepeople .... a very dangerous life. (have)

There .... many wild animals. (be)

If they .... an animal (see), they .... a terrible sound (make).

They .... after the animals and killed them.(go)

Revision box Comparatives and superlatives

1 Can you complete the sentence? Write seven different sentences using the adjectives a–g.
   Life is .... now but 15,000 years ago it was ....
   a hard b quiet c easy d difficult e short f good g bad

2 Can you complete the sentence? Write five different sentences using the adjectives a–e.
   A giraffe is .... but an elephant is probably the .... animal in the world.
   a strong b big c fat d heavy e beautiful

3 Work with a partner. Do you know any 'tallest/biggest/ strongest/fastest' facts?
   Write as many as you can. Use these words.
   tall *The tallest mountain in the world is Mount Everest.*
   fast short good (the best) bad (the worst) expensive (the most expensive)
   small high deep long heavy strong

   Compare your facts with other students in your class. Who has the most?

31 Activity
A book about your family and friends

Before your lesson

Step 1 When were they born? What did they do?

Find out some information about your family and friends – your mother, father, grandparents, brothers, sisters, uncles, aunts, cousins:

when they were born	where they lived	how many children they had
where they were born	when they got married	their jobs

Find some old or recent photographs of your family and friends.
You also need some glue, scissors and some paper to make a small book.

In your lesson

Step 2
Your family tree

Draw your family tree.
Write some sentences to describe the people on your family tree.
Don't forget yourself!

You can write about:

when they were born
where they were born
their job
something interesting
   about them.

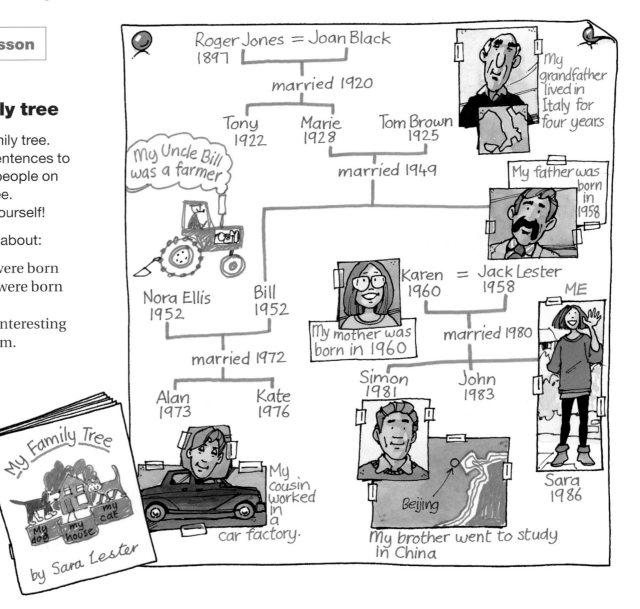

Roger Jones = Joan Black
1897
married 1920

Tony 1922   Marie 1928   Tom Brown 1925
married 1949

My Uncle Bill was a farmer

My grandfather lived in Italy for four years

My father was born in 1958

Nora Ellis 1952   Bill 1952

Karen 1960 = Jack Lester 1958
ME
married 1980

My mother was born in 1960

married 1972

Alan 1973   Kate 1976

Simon 1981   John 1983

Sara 1986

My Family Tree
my dog my house my cat
by Sara Lester

My cousin worked in a car factory.

Beijing

My brother went to study in China

Step 3 **Write about some more people**

Write some more information about some other people you know. Put their photographs in your book.

My grandmother was born in 1938. She lived in Mexico for 20 years. She was a nurse. She had 6 children. Her name is Isabel. She lives with her brother about 2 kilometres from our house.

This is my brother. His name is David. He is 1 year old. He was born last year. He walked in the garden yesterday. He cries a lot. He is very nice but he takes my things.

This is my friend. Her name is Alicia. She is 13 years old. She was born in America but now she lives here. She likes swimming and she can play the piano. We often go out on our bikes together.

Step 4 **Show your books to each other**

When you finish, sit in small groups and look at each other's books.
Read and talk about what you have done.

Step 5 **How you learn: evaluation**

Discuss these questions with people in your class.

Which part of your family and friends book was most difficult to write?
What did you learn about your family and friends?
What more can you put in your book?

32 Culture matters
Living traditions

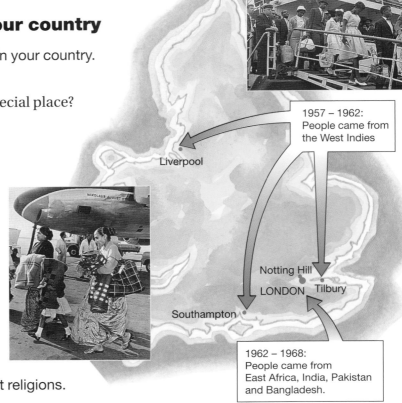

1 Your ideas Celebrations in your country

Think about the important events you celebrate in your country.
What are they?

> Do you have special food? Do you meet in a special place?
> Do you have parties? Do you give presents?
> Do different groups of people celebrate
> different events?

Look at the celebrations
in this unit. Do you have
any celebrations like this?

1957 – 1962:
People came from
the West Indies

Liverpool

Notting Hill

LONDON Tilbury

Southampton

1962 – 1968:
People came from
East Africa, India, Pakistan
and Bangladesh.

2 People in Britain
Who has celebrations in Britain?

In Britain there are many different celebrations.
The people who live in Britain come from
many different countries and have many different religions.

3 Reading When are the celebrations?

📼 There are celebrations every month in Britain.
Read about them and write the name in the correct month.
You can listen to the texts.

Jan	
Feb	
Mar	
Apr	
May	
Jun	
July	
Aug	
Sept	
Oct	
Nov	
Dec	

THE NOTTING HILL CARNIVAL
Between 1956 and 1962 the British government
asked people from the Caribbean to come to
England. They worked in the hospitals and on
trains and buses in London. Now every August
in London there is a big carnival with music in
the streets of Notting Hill.

DIWALI

Between 1962 and 1968 many people from India and Pakistan came to live and work in Britain. Their most important celebration every year is Diwali. This is a big festival of lights and dancing with special food and new clothes. Diwali is usually between September and November.

CHRISTMAS DAY

On December 25th, Christmas Day, people give presents, send cards and eat a special dinner at home. The children are usually very excited because they get presents from Father Christmas (Santa Claus). In their houses, people have a special tree with lights.

CHINESE NEW YEAR

Like Diwali, this celebration moves its date each year. Usually it is in January or February. In many big cities the people build paper dragons. wear masks and have fireworks, lights and music in the street.

GUY FAWKES NIGHT

In November, the most important celebration is 'Guy Fawkes Night'. On November 5, 1605, a man called Guy Fawkes tried to blow up the Houses of Parliament. He failed and, since then, people celebrate it. They light fireworks and big fires. It is usually very cold!

EID AL FITR

At Eid, Muslim children wear new clothes and the adults give them presents, sweets and money. Everyone has a family party with special food.

4 Reading What is a celebration?

Work in a small group. What do people do for each celebration in Exercise 3? Put a tick (✓) in the chart.

Now think about a celebration in your country and fill in the chart. Tell the other students in your class about the celebration.

	CARNIVAL	DIWALI	GUY FAWKES	CHRISTMAS	CHINESE NEW YEAR	EID	YOUR CELEBRATION
1 Eat special foods							
2 Give presents							
3 Wear new clothes							
4 Send cards							
5 Visit people							
6 Go on the streets							
7 Stay at home							
8 Have a party							
9 Dance							
10 Sing							

33 Revision and evaluation
Units 29–32

1 Self-assessment How much do you know?

How well do you think you know the
English you learned in Units 29–32?
Put a tick (✓) in the box.

Now do sections 2–6.

	very well	OK	a little
'was' and 'were'			
The Past tense ('-ed' verbs)			
The Past ('went, made, had', etc.)			
Talk about past events			
New words			

2 An example test Test yourself

How much do you know? Work with your neighbour.
When you have finished, check your answers on page 144.
Look back at Exercise 1. Were you right?

TEST YOURSELF

A Grammar 'was/were'

Fill in the gaps in this text with 'was' or 'were'.

We know that cavepeople ......1...... good artists. But they ......2...... also good
musicians. Their pipes ......3...... animal bones.

The leg bone ......4...... the best pipe. When the bone ......5...... dry, the cavepeople
made some holes in it. When the pipe ......6...... ready, they played some music.

B Writing Write about the past

Use these verbs to write about what
Anna did at the weekend.

Saturday	Sunday
television (watch)	car (clean)
mother (help)	friend (talk)
a cake (make)	a film (see)

*On Saturday, Anna watched
television. Then she ...*

C Vocabulary What's the word?

Find the word in the square. They go across and down.

1

2 Cavepeople painted p....................

3 r....................

4 Cavepeople h....................
for their food.

5 They killed the animals
with s....................

6 u....................
d....................

A	B	D	C	A	V	E	H	J	J	K	U	N
G	T	E	F	E	T	R	E	Y	O	A	J	H
U	P	S	I	D	E	A	D	O	W	N	E	U
R	A	J	K	E	U	H	J	E	V	M	A	N
I	W	S	P	E	A	R	S	Q	P	M	A	T
V	S	H	W	J	U	A	N	Q	D	K	M	E
E	A	P	I	C	T	U	R	E	S	Y	W	D
R	K	J	O	K	E	O	M	H	A	G	F	E

D Writing Past simple

Write five sentences about the life of someone you know well – a friend, a famous person or someone in your family or yourself!

3 Do it yourself! Write your own test

Work in small groups. Look back at Units 29 to 32 and write part of a test for your class. Look at Exercise 2 for ideas. Tell your teacher which section you are doing.

A 'was/were'   **B** New words   **C** Past tense verbs   **D** Write about the Past tense

Give the test to your teacher to check and put together for your class.

4 How do you learn Evaluation

4.1 Discussion Talk about your English work

First, with your class, decide which groups will look at Unit 29 or Unit 30 or Unit 31 or Unit 32.

Work in a group of three or four students. Decide who will report back to the class.
Look through the Units you chose and talk about these questions.

Unit 29 groups
 Did you think the topic was interesting?
 Did you have enough time do the exercises?

Unit 30 groups
 Were the grammar presentations clear?
 Which grammar point was the most difficult / the easiest?

Unit 31 groups
 Which activity did you enjoy most?
 Was it difficult to write about your family and friends?

Unit 32 groups
 What traditions did you find most interesting?
 Did you have enough time to read all the texts?

4.2 Your own ideas Write what you think

Write down what *you* think. Give your paper to your teacher at the end of the lesson.

5 Writing Write a letter to us!

Help us to write the books that you want. Tell us what you liked and what you didn't like in the book!

Before you write your letter, work in small groups and discuss your ideas about the book. Talk about these parts of the book:

> the *Topic* Units
> the *Language focus* Units
> the *Activities*
> the *Culture matters* Units
> the *Exercise Box*
> the *Ideas list*
> the *Language Records*
> the songs
> the games
> the Workbook

Useful words:

> easy   difficult   just right
> boring   interesting
> fast   slow

Write the letter alone or in your group. Send it to this address:

Or send a fax to:

> ++ 44 1223 325984

Or send an e-mail message to:

> aldh@cup.cam.ac.uk

Many thanks!

Dear Andrew and Diana,

We are class.........in.........
..........School in ....
and we are using...................
We think...............

AIR MAIL

Andrew Littlejohn and Diana Hicks
c/o Cambridge University Press
ELT Group
The Edinburgh Building
Shaftesbury Road
Cambridge CB2 2RU
England

Answers to the test in Exercise 2

C The words are: cave, pictures, river, hunted, spears, upside down.

B On Saturday, Anna watched television. Then she helped her mother and made a cake. On Sunday, she cleaned the car and talked to a friend. She also saw a film.

A 1 were 2 were 3 were 4 were 5 was 6 was

Theme trail **A revision game**

What you need

Four counters and a dice:

Aim

To answer correctly three questions from Topic Units
and three questions from Language focus Units.

To get to 'Home'.

How to play

1 Play in a group of three or four people. One person is the Questioner
and only he/she can look at the questions on page 148.
2 Put your counter anywhere on the board.
3 Roll the dice and move your counter.
4 The Questioner will ask you a question about the Unit where you are on the board.
5 If you get the answer right tick the Progress Chart below.
6 Go round the board until you have a correct answer for three Topic Units and three
Language focus Units.
7 To finish, continue to throw the dice and answer questions until you get the right
number to reach 'Home'.
The first person to finish is the winner.

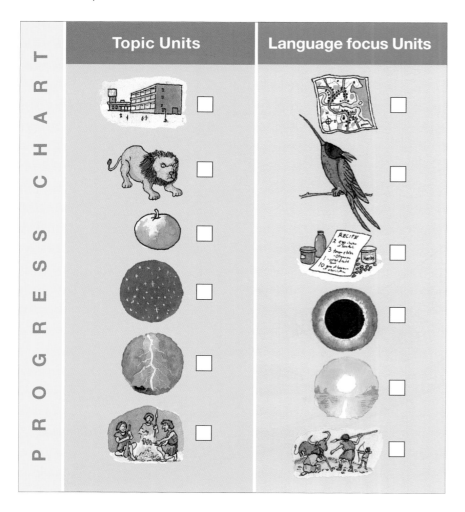

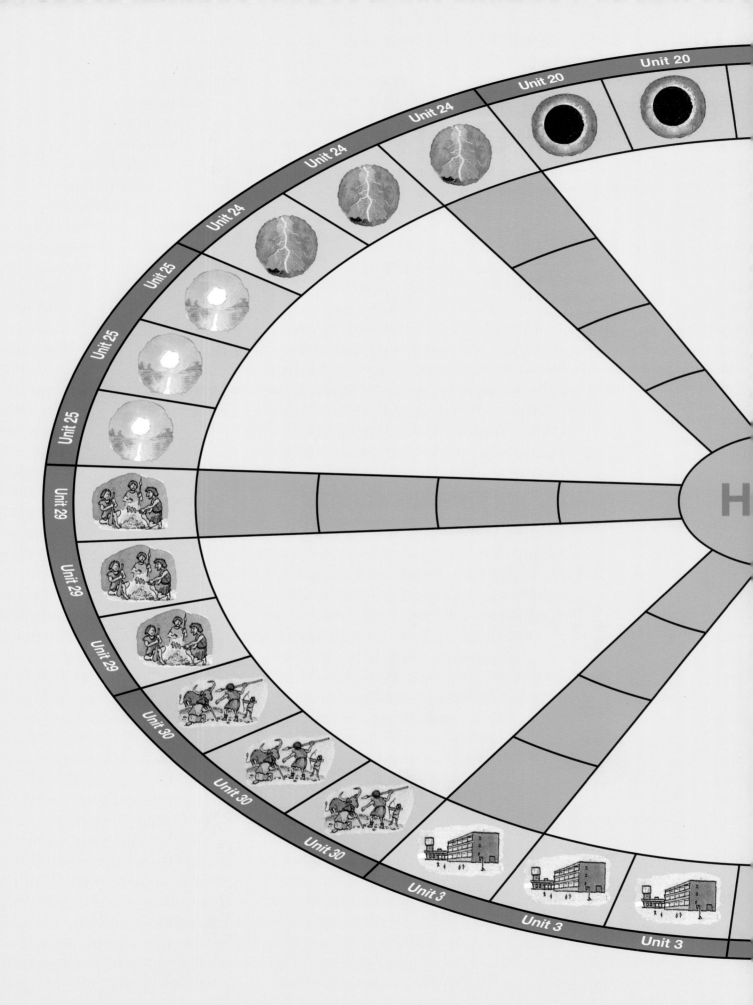

Unit 20

Unit 20

Unit 24

Unit 24

Unit 24

Unit 25

Unit 25

Unit 25

Unit 29

Unit 29

Unit 29

Unit 30

Unit 30

Unit 30

Unit 3

Unit 3

Unit 3

H

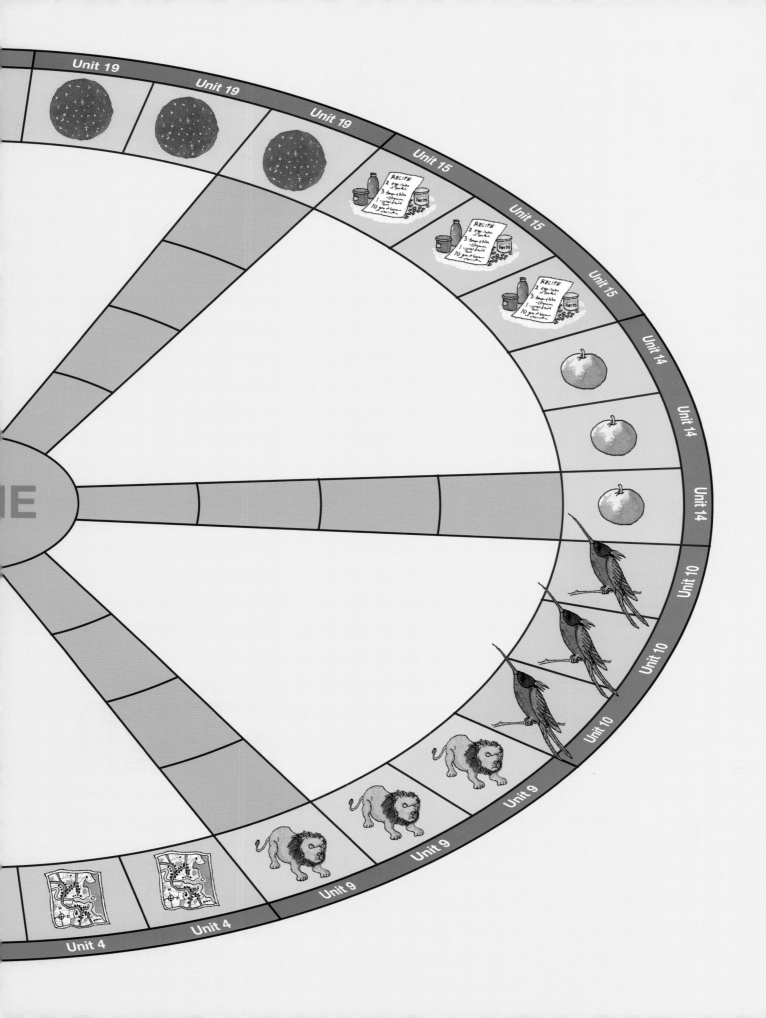

Theme trail Questions

UNIT 3

1 Is your town in the north of the country?
2 Are there any flats near your school?
3 How do you come to school?
4 What subjects do you have on Tuesday morning?

UNIT 4

1 Are these words nouns, verbs or adjectives?
   cold big town sleep
2 Put this sentence in the right order:
   not school music I at study do
3 Say two things that you **don't** do.
4 Say two things that you can say in a shop.

UNIT 9

1 What is a mammal?
2 What is a reptile?
3 Say two things about giraffes.
4 Where do elephants live?

UNIT 10

1 Ask two questions about pandas.
2 What are the questions?
.... They sleep at night.
.... They eat bamboo.
.... They live in China.
3 What is the possessive adjective?
   This is ...*my*... bag.
   I → ..*my*...   you → ....   he → ....   she → ....
   it → ....   we → ....   they → ....
4 Say two things you can say when you make a new friend.

UNIT 14

1 Say three important things that are in food (Carbohydrates...).
2 Say one that you have for breakfast, one thing you have for lunch and one thing you have for dinner.
3 What food has lots of fibre?
4 Why are fats important in food?

UNIT 15

1 'Some' or 'any'?
   We've got .... butter but we haven't got
   .... eggs.
   Have you got .... eggs?
2 Complete the sentences.
   Vitamins are important. We need them.
   That's Peter. Do you know ....?
   This is my new bike. Do you like ....?
   There's Mona. Can you see ....?
3 When do you use 'some'? When do you use 'any'?
4 What is the object pronoun?
   She gave it to ....*me*.. .
   I → ..*me*...   you → ....   he → ....   she → ....
   it → ....   we → ....   they → ....

UNIT 19

1 'The sky is history'. Why?
2 What does the moon do to the Earth?
3 How is the moon different from Earth?
4 Which is the smallest planet? Which is the hottest planet? Which planet is nearest to the sun?

UNIT 20

1 Say three things that people are doing NOW where you are.
2 You are in a bus station. You want to know which bus goes to the next town, East Town, the price of the ticket and the times. What do you say?
3 Say three tallest/fastest/biggest/smallest sentences. The biggest city in the world is Mexico City.
4 What can you say about New Zealand, England and Saudi Arabia?

New Zealand 8°   England 20°   Saudi Arabia 40°

UNIT 24

1 Why do we have winds?
2 Why do we have rain?
3 How is the weather different in December and June in your country?
4 Warm air .... but cold air ....

UNIT 25

1 Complete the sentences with 'much' or 'many':
   a I don't have .... money.
   b Do you know .... people here?
   c We have .... windy days in December.
2 Are these things 'countable' or 'uncountable'?
   water books air pencils sheep butter
3 What plans do you have for next week? Say three things.
   On Monday, I'm ...
4 What can you say about these cars?

UNIT 29

1 When did cavepeople live in caves?
2 What jobs did the cave children do?
3 Say four differences between life today and cave life.
4 Which animals the cavepeople hunt?

UNIT 30

1 What is the past of 'walk' and 'talk'?
2 What is the past of 'go' and 'have'?
3 Say two things that you did yesterday.
4 A friend went to a party last night. What can you ask him/her about it?

'Danger' cards

These are the cards for the Exercise 8.1 game on page 129.

4 An elephant attacked you. Go to 1.	**5** You were ill. Go to 2.	**8** You talked to a friend. Miss a turn.	**2** It rained very hard. Miss a turn.	**7** A tiger chased you. Go to 4.	**10** You killed a bear. Go to 12.
3 You picked a lot of fruit on trees. Go to 8.	**6** A dangerous person from another group chased you. Go back to 2.	**9** You went into the river. Miss a turn.	**1** You went to a party at another cave. Miss a turn.	**4** You had some bad fruit. Go to 2.	**8** You went fishing all day. Go to 5.

'Danger' rules

How to play

You need a dice and four counters.

1 Play in a group of four. Choose a path. Put your counter at the start.

2 Read the 'Danger' cards on page 149. Write one more.
   – If you are 'Yellow', write a card for Red square 13.
   – If you are 'Red', write a card for Green square 11.
   – If you are 'Green', write a card for Blue square 12.
   – If you are 'Blue', write a card for Yellow square 11.
   Put your card on the table.

3 Throw the dice and move forwards.
   If you land on a DANGER square, read the card. Do what it says.

4 When you get to the cave, throw the dice again.
   If you get 1, 2, or 3, say two things which happened to you.
   If you get 4, 5 or 6, say three things which happened to you.

The first person to get to the cave and to say the two or three things is the winner!

Ideas list

Here are some ideas to help you make your own exercises. (Remember to put the answers and your name on the back of your card.)

Ideas

Examples

Idea 1 Word halves

Choose some words and cut them in half.

   football
   picnic
   timetable
   geography
   language

What are the words?

pic   uage
lang   table
geog   ball
foot   nic
time   raphy

Idea 2 Put the letters in the right order

Choose some words and mix up the letters.

   football   factories   picnic   timetable
   geography   language

What are the words?

   casioftre albofotl icpcin meibalett
   haoggrepy aaeulngg

Idea 3 Put the words in the right order

Choose some sentences and mix up the words.

   How much is this cassette?
   Let's go to the newsagents.
   I don't walk to school.

What are the sentences?

   1 is much cassette how this ?
   2 the lets to newsagents go
   3 walk I school don't to

Idea 4 Match the words with the pictures or the meaning

Choose some words and draw some pictures or write the meaning in your language.

flat	school
cassette	picnic
picnic	timetable
school	cassette
timetable	flat
Science	Science

Match the words with the pictures or the meaning.

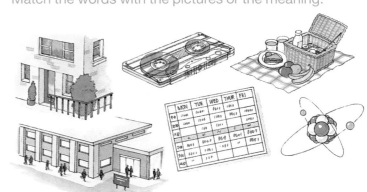

Idea 5 Find the words

Choose some words and hide them in a square of letters. Write some clues.

blue	Find the words.
radio	1 The colour of the sky.
television	2 Something to listen to.
red	3 Something to watch.
green	4 The colour that says 'Stop!'
England	5 The colour of leaves.
flat	6 London is the capital of ....
black	7 I don't live in a house. I live in a ....
	8 The colour of the sky at night.

```
R  E  D  T (B  L  U  E) Y  U  F
S  G  R  E  E  N  B  N  M  K  L
R  A  D  I  O  E  L  L  O  W  A
C  V  B  N  M  B  R  T  E  N  T
E  N  G  L  A  N  D  U  I  O  P
D  C  B  L  A  C  K  G  G  B  F
T  E  L  E  V  I  S  I  O  N  U
```

Idea 6 Put the sentences in the right order

Choose a dialogue or a paragraph. Mix up the sentences.

MONA: Hello. What's your name?
SOPHIE: Sophie. What's your name?
MONA: Mona. Do you want a sweet?
SOPHIE: Thanks.
MONA: Do you want to play volleyball?
SOPHIE: I don't know how to play.
MONA: It's easy. I can show you.
SOPHIE: OK. Let's go.

Put the sentences in the right order.

– It's easy. I can show you.
– Do you want to play volleyball?
– Hello. What's your name?
– Thanks.
– I don't know how to play.
– OK. Let's go.
– Sophie. What's your name?
– Mona. Do you want a sweet?

Idea 7 What's the question?

Write some questions and answers. Copy the answers.
Leave space for the questions.

1 Where do you live?

   In Prospect Street.

2 What's your telephone number?

   We haven't got a telephone.

3 Do you want a chocolate?

   No, thanks. I don't like chocolate.

What's the question?

1 ....?

   In Prospect Street.

2 ....?

   We haven't got a telephone.

3 ....?

   No, thanks. I don't like chocolate.

Idea 8 Fill in the missing words

Choose a paragraph and take out some words.

Many people in England spend a lot of their free time
in the country. There are 10 very big national parks
and people from the towns like to go there. Some
people go walking or have a picnic. Other people
do different sports.

Fill in the missing words.

Many people .... England spend a lot of their free time
in .... country. There .... 10 very big national parks
and people .... the towns like to go there. Some .... go
walking or have a picnic. Other people do .... sports.

Idea 9 Answer the questions

Choose a paragraph and write some questions.

Many people in England spend a lot of their free time
in the country. There are 10 very big national parks
and people from the towns like to go there. Some
people go walking or have a picnic. Other people
do different sports.

Answer the questions.

1 Where do English people spend a lot of time?
2 How many national parks are there?
3 What do people do in the national parks?

Idea 10 True or false?

Choose a paragraph and write some true
and untrue sentences.

Many people in England spend a lot of their free time
in the country. There are 10 very big national parks
and people from the towns like to go there. Some
people go walking or have a picnic. Other people
do different sports.

Are these sentences true, false or is the information
not in the text?

1 Everybody in England likes the country.
2 There are many rivers in the parks.
3 There are more than 20 big national parks in England.
4 Some people have picnics in the national parks.

Useful sets

The alphabet (by sound)

/eɪ/	/iː/	/e/	/aɪ/	/əʊ/	/juː/	/ɑː/
a	b	f	i	o	q	r
h	c	l	y		u	
j	d	m			w	
k	e	n				
	g	s				
	p	x				
	t	z				
	v					

Irregular verbs

Infinitive	Past simple	Past participle
be	was, were	been
become	became	become
buy	bought	bought
can	could	—
come	came	come
do	did	done
draw	drew	drawn
eat	ate	eaten
find	found	found
get	got	got
go	went	gone
have	had	had
leave	left	left
make	made	made
meet	met	met
put	put	put
run	ran	run
say	said	said
see	saw	seen
sell	sold	sold
sit	sat	sat
speak	spoke	spoken
take	took	taken
tell	told	told
think	thought	thought
understand	understood	understood
wake	woke	woken
wear	wore	worn
write	wrote	written

Subjects

English
Mathematics
Geography
History

Science
(Chemistry,
Physics,
Biology)

Sports
Games
Religion

Numbers

1 one   2 two   3 three   4 four   5 five   6 six   7 seven   8 eight
9 nine   10 ten   11 eleven   12 twelve   13 thirteen   14 fourteen
15 fifteen   16 sixteen   17 seventeen   18 eighteen   19 nineteen
20 twenty

31 thirty-one   42 forty-two   53 fifty-three   64 sixty-four
75 seventy-five   86 eighty-six   97 ninety-seven   100 a hundred
201 two hundred and one   1,000 a thousand   10,000 ten
thousand   1,000,000 a million

Colours

Rainbow colours

red   orange   yellow   green   blue   indigo   violet

Primary colours

red   yellow   blue   green

Other colours

white   black   purple   pink   brown

Colour adjectives

pale/light
bright
dark
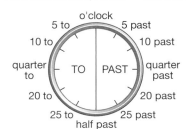

Times and dates

January 7th, 1997 – 'January the seventh, nineteen ninety seven'
December 8th, 2000 – 'December the eighth, two thousand'

It's twenty-five to four.

It's a quarter past eight.

Days

Monday
Tuesday
Wednesday
Thursday

Friday
Saturday
Sunday

Months

January
February
March
April
May
June

July
August
September
October
November
December

Map of the world

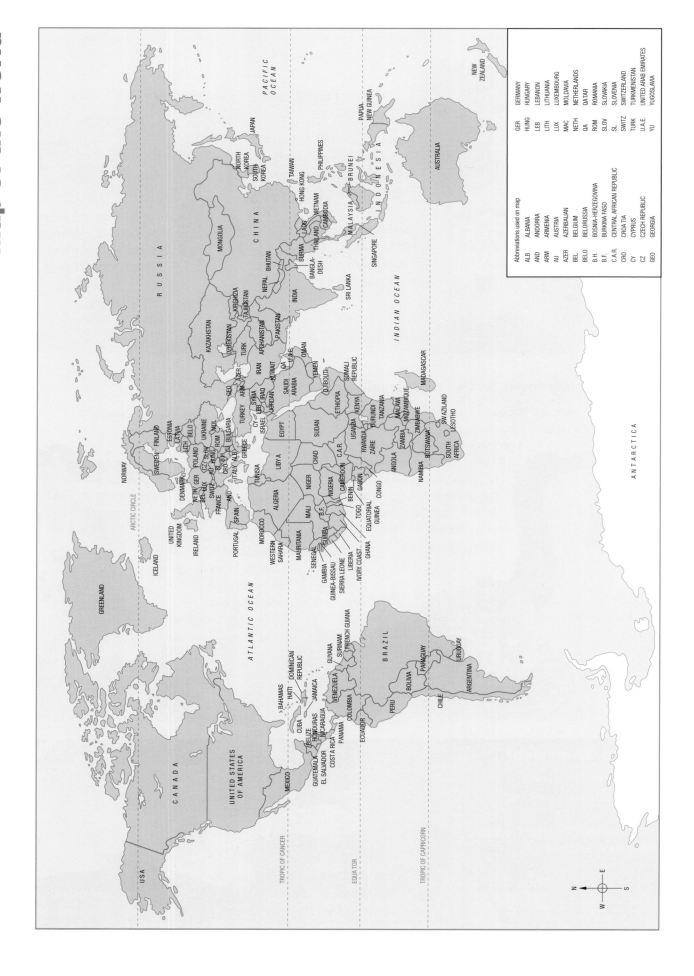

Songs

Unit 1 'I'm so happy'

I've got lots of friends
in my school.
I've got lots of friends
in my town.
I've got lots of
things to do.
I've got lots of
things to say.

I'm so happy,
Life's so good.
I'm so happy,
Life's so good.

There is music in my house.
There is music in my school.
There is sunshine in my street.
There is sunshine in my town.

I'm so happy,
Life's so good.
I'm so happy,
Life's so good.

I've got lots of friends in my school.
I've got lots of friends in my town.
I've got lots of things to do.
I've got lots of things to say.

I'm so happy,
Life's so good.

Unit 3 'In my town, in the countryside'

In my town there are shops
And there's a railway station.
I go there and I buy
A ticket for my destination.
I'm going to the countryside,
I'm going to the countryside.
I love it, I love it, I love it.
Birds and hills and big blue skies,
In the countryside

In the countryside there are farms,
There are animals too.
But all my friends live in my town
So this is what I do:
I go back to my town,
I go back to my town.
I love it, I love it, I love it.
Cars and people all around,
In my town.
I love it, I love it, I love it.
Birds and hills and
big blue skies,
In the countryside. *etc.*

Unit 9 'Wimoweh'

Wimoweh, wimoweh,
Wimoweh, wimoweh, etc.

In the jungle, the mighty jungle,
The lion sleeps tonight.

In the jungle the mighty fire,
The fire burns bright tonight.

Hush my darling,
Don't cry my darling,
The lion sleeps tonight.

Wimoweh, wimoweh,
Wimoweh, wimoweh, etc.

Unit 14 'I love chocolate'

I drink milk, I eat cheese,
I like nuts and I like greens,
I like cereals, I like beans,
These are things my body needs.

Chorus
But late at night,
Under my bedclothes,
I eat chocolate,
And no-one knows.

I eat vegetables, I drink juice,
I like rice, I like fruit,
I like pasta every way,
I eat good things every day.

Repeat chorus

I like honey on my bread,
I like salad and I like eggs,
I drink water all day long,
All these things make me strong.

Repeat chorus

Unit 19 'Space'

In the night, night sky
I can see
Bright, bright lights
Are shining on you and me,
And in the bright, bright lights
There are creatures too,
In their night, night skies,
They're looking at me and you.

Chorus
The moon, the stars, the universe,
It's a beautiful place,
The planets and the galaxies,
Space, space, space.

So tonight, night, night,
Now you know,
Look at the bright, bright lights,
Look up and say 'Hello'.

Repeat chorus

Every night, I say 'Hi'
To my neighbours in the sky,
Every night I sing my song,
Everybody sing along:

I live on Planet Zaarb,
Can anybody hear?
I live on planet Zaarb,
Does anyone know I'm here?

Final chorus
The moon, the stars, the universe,
It's a beautiful place,
The planets and the galaxies,
I live out here in, space, space!

Unit 24 'Singing in the rain'

I'm singing in the rain,
Just singing in the rain,
What a glorious feeling,
I'm happy again,
I'm laughing at clouds,
So dark up above,
The sun's in my heart
And I'm ready for love.

Let the stormy clouds chase
Everyone from the place,
Come on with the rain
I've a smile on my face,
I walk down the lane,
With a happy refrain,
Just singing, just singing
In the rain.

I'm singing and dancing in the rain,
I'm dancing and singing in the rain.

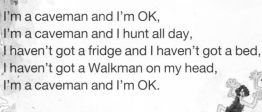

Unit 29 'Caveman rock'

I'm a caveman and I'm OK,
I'm a caveman and I hunt all day,
I haven't got a car and I haven't got a flat,
I haven't got a dog or a pussy cat,
I'm a caveman and I'm OK.

I'm a caveman and I'm OK,
I'm a caveman and I hunt all day,
I keep my paint inside a bone,
I cut my meat with spears and stone,
I'm a caveman and I'm OK.

I'm a caveman and I'm OK,
I'm a caveman and I hunt all day,
I haven't got a fridge and I haven't got a bed,
I haven't got a Walkman on my head,
I'm a caveman and I'm OK.

I'm a caveman and I'm OK,
I'm a caveman and I hunt all day,
I keep quite warm with fire and skin,
I make the pots that we cook in,
I'm a caveman and I'm OK.

Wordlist/Index

In this list you can find the words which appear in the *Topic*, *Language focus* and *Culture matters* Units and their page numbers. This list is also an index of the parts of the book and the grammar in the book.

Abbreviations:
adj. adjective   *adv.* adverb   *conj.* conjunction
interj. interjection   *n.* noun   *obj. pron.* object pronoun
pl. plural   *poss. adj.* possessive adjective   *prep.* preposition
sing. singular   *subj. pron.* subject pronoun   *v.* verb

Thanks and acknowledgements

Authors' thanks

The development of this course has been a large part of our lives for well over six years. During this time, we have become indebted to literally thousands of people who have so generously shared their time, skills and experience. In particular, we appreciate the constructive advice of the numerous teachers and students who helped with our initial classroom research and with the piloting, the readers, and the language teaching specialists. The final version owes much to their enthusiastic involvement.

We would like to record a special 'thank you' to Peter Donovan, who shared our ideals of innovation and who has provided input and support throughout. Also to James Dingle, our editor, whose hard work, professionalism, understanding and painstaking attention to detail have helped transform our ideals into reality and Sarah Brierley who so efficiently managed the production of the pilot edition, and for her help on the final materials. For skilled editorial support in producing this 'new look' edition we are indebted to Meredith Levy, and also to Maria Pylas, to whom we owe our most sincere thanks.

We would also like to thank the Cambridge University Press sales managers and representatives around the world for all their help and support.

Finally, from Andrew, a tribute to Lita, Daniel, Fiona and David for their support and inspiration. From Diana, a big 'thank you' to Tom, Sam and Tara. Thank you for waiting so long.

Andrew Littlejohn   *Diana Hicks*

The authors and publishers would like to thank the following individuals for their vital support throughout the project:

Professor Michael Breen, Edith Cowan University, Perth, Australia; Jeff Stranks, Cultura Inglesa, Rio de Janeiro, Brazil; Laura Izarra, OSEC, São Paulo, Brazil; Sergio de Souza Gabriel, Cultura Inglesa, São Paulo, Brazil; Françoise Motard, France; Eleni Miltsakaki, Athens, Greece; Akis Davanellos, The Davanellos School of Languages, Lamia, Greece; Paola Zambonelli, SMS Volta, Bologna, Italy; Cristina Zanoni, SMS Pepoli, Bologna, Italy; Emilia Paloni, SMS Lorenzo Milani, Caivano, Italy; Gisella Langé, Legnano, Italy; Mariella Merli, Milan, Italy; Roberta Fachinetti, SMS Mastri Caravaggini, Caravaggio, Italy; Giovanna Carella, SMS Nazarino Sauro, Novate Milanese, Italy; Dominique Bertrand, SMS Giacomo Leopardi, Rome, Italy; Jan Hague, British Council, Rome, Italy; Val Benson, Suzugamine (Joshi Tandai), Hiroshima, Japan; Małgorzata Szwaj, English Unlimited, Gdańsk, Poland; Alistair MacLean, NKJO, Krosno, Poland; Janina Rybienik, Przemyśl, Poland; Hanna Kijowska, Warsaw, Poland; Ewa Kołodziejska, Warsaw, Poland; Zeynep Çağlar, Beyoğlu Anadolu Lisesi, Istanbul, Turkey; Maureen Günkut, Turkey; Steve Cooke, UK.

The authors and publishers would like to thank the following institutions for their help in testing the material and for the invaluable feedback which they provided:

Colegio Sion, Rio de Janeiro, Brazil; Open English House, Curitiba, Brazil; Ginásio Integrado Madalena Khan, Leblon, Brazil; Steps in English Curso Ltda., Niterói, Brazil; Instituto Educacional Stella Maris, Rio de Janeiro, Brazil; Cultura Inglesa, São Carlos, Brazil; Colegio Bandeirantes, São Paulo, Brazil; Kaumeya Language School, Alexandria, Egypt; Victory College, Victoria, Egypt; Collège Jean Jaures, Aire-sur-la-Lys, France; Collège Louis Le Prince-Ringuet, La Fare-les-Oliviers, France; Collège de Misedon, Port Brillet, France; The Aidonoupolou School, Athens, Greece; the following language school owners in Greece: Petros Dourtourekas, Athens; Eleni Fakalou, Athens; Angeliki & Lance Kinnick, Athens; Mark Palmer, Athens; Georgia Stamatopoulou, Athens; Anna Zerbini-Vasiliadou, Athens; Shirley Papanikolaou, Heraklion; Tony Hatzinikolaou, Kos; Antonis Trechas, Piraeus; SMS Italo Calvino, Milan, Italy; SMS G Rodari, Novate Milanese, Italy; SMS L Fibonacci, Pisa, Italy; Accademia Britannica/International House, Rome, Italy; David English House, Hiroshima, Japan; British Council, Tokyo, Japan; Senri International School, Japan; Szkoła Podstawowa w Bratkówce, Poland; Primary School, Debowiec, Poland; 4th Independent Primary School, Kraków, Poland; Gama Bell School of English, Kraków, Poland; Kosmopolita, Łódź, Poland; Private Language School PRIME, Łódź, Poland; Szkoła Społeczna 2001, Łódź, Poland; Szkoła Podstawowa Nr 11, Nowy Sacz, Poland; Omnibus, Poznań, Poland; Szkoła Jezyków Obcych J. Rybienik i A. Ochalskiej, Przemyśl, Poland; Szkoła Podstawowa Nr 23, Warsaw, Poland; Szkoła Podstawowa Nr 320, Warsaw, Poland; Liceum Ogólnokształcace Wschowa, Poland; Yukselis Koleji I, Ankara, Turkey; Özel Kalamiş Lisesi, Istanbul, Turkey; Özel Şener Lisesi, Istanbul, Turkey.

The authors and publishers would like to thank the following for all their help in the production of the finished materials:

Marcus Askwith: freelance design work; Broadway School, Birmingham: help with the *Out and about* photographs. Particular thanks to Martyn Bennett and the children who participated; Peter Ducker: pilot edition design; Gecko Limited, Bicester, Oxon: all stages of design and production. Particular thanks to David Evans, James Arnold, Wendy Homer, Linda Beveridge & Sharon Ryan; Goodfellow & Egan, Cambridge: four-colour scanning and film. Particular thanks to David Ward; Steve Hall of Bell Voice Recordings: recording and production of the songs; Heather Richards: help with selecting artists; Janet and Peter Simmonett: freelance design work; Tim Wharton: writing and performing of songs; Martin Williamson (Prolingua Productions), Diana and Peter Thompson (Studio AVP) and all of the actors who contributed to the recorded material.

The authors and publishers are grateful to the following for permission to record the music and reproduce the words of the following songs:

Wimoweh (The Lion Sleeps Tonight) (words on p. 154): words and music by George David Weiss, Hugo Peretti and Luigi Creatore. Copyright © 1961. Renewed 1989 and assigned to Abilene Music Inc. Administered by The Songwriters Guild of America. Rights for the world, excluding the United States and Canada, controlled by Memory Lane Music Limited, London. All rights reserved – international copyright secured – reprinted by permission. *Singing in the Rain* (words on p. 155): CPP/Belwin Europe (words) and EMI (music).

In My Town, In The Countryside, I Love Chocolate and *Space*: words and music by Tim Wharton. *I'm So Happy* and *Caveman Rock*: words by Andrew Littlejohn & Diana Hicks, music by Tim Wharton.

The authors and publishers are grateful to the following illustrators and photographic sources:

Illustrators: Sophie Allington: pp. 45 *tr*, 46 *t*, 47, 48, 66; Alex Ayliffe: pp. 85 *ml*, 102, 103, 113; Felicity Roma Bowers: pp. 45 *br*, 49, 53, 85 *mr*, 98 *b*, 99, 105 *bl*, 106, 107 *t & b*; Maggie Brand: pp. 68 *b*, 73, 76, 83 *t*, 122; Robert Calow: pp. 10, 14 *t*, 17 *t*, 24, 38, 60 *t*, 92, 100, 140; Richard Deverell: pp. 56, 75, 101, 109, 117, 150; Hilary Evans: handwritten items; Gecko Limited: all DTP illustrations and graphics; Peter Kent: pp. 6 *b*, 7 *b*, 23 *tl & bl*, 25, 26 *b*, 36, 40, 60 *b*, 74, 81, 108, 114, 123, 129, 145, 146, 147, 148; Steve Lach: pp. 20, 23 *tr*, 43; Jan Lewis: illustration for *Language Records*; Pat Ludlow: pp. 11 *t*, 17 *b*, 135, 136, 142; Colin Mier: pp. 54, 55, 67, 82, 94, 97; John Plumb: pp. 11 *b*, 12 *t*, 28 *t*, 78, 79, 87 *m*, 98 *t*, 105 *tl*, 119, 125 *bl*, 126 *b*, 127 *b*, 130 *b*, 138, 139; Debbie Ryder: pp. 12 *b*, 27, 47 *b*, 70, 88 *t*, 107 *m*, 128 *t*, 154, 155; Chris Ryley: pp. 6 *tr*, 17 *c*, 18, 42, 63, 65, 83 *b*, 125 *tr*, 126 *t*, 127 *t*, 128 *b*, 130 *b*, 133, 134, 143; John Storey: pp. 14 *b*, 15, 16, 45 *bl*, 61, 85 *t*, 86, 87 *t & b*, 88 *b*, 89, 93; Sam Thompson: p. 68 *t*; Angela Wood: p. 69; Mel Wright: pp. 19, 26 *t*, 28 *b*, 125 *m*, 144.

Photographic sources: Art Directors Photo Library: pp. 6 *mr*, 125 *br*, 141 *cr*; Aspect Picture Library: pp. 6 *t*, 86; Aspect Picture Library/ Derek Bayes: p. 141 *bl*; Aspect Picture Library/Peter Carmichael: pp. 6 *br*, 24 *mr*, 100 *bcl*; Aspect Picture Library/Les Dyson: p. 62 *b*; Barnabys Picture Library: pp. 23 *cl*, 38 *br*; 'Big Pit Mining Museum', Blaenafon, Gwent, South Wales: p. 39 *tl*; Erich Bach/Britstock–IFA: p. 24 *t*; The J. Allan Cash Photolibrary: pp. 19, 38 *bc*, 46 *bcl*, 92, 93 *l & r*; Bruce Coleman Limited/Bob and Clara Calhoun: p. 52 *cr*; Bruce Coleman Limited/Rod Williams: pp. 52 *tr*; Clifford Colwell: pp. 58 *l*, 59 *tl*; 'Commission for the New Towns': pp. 38 *t*, 39 *cr*; © 1995 Comstock Inc.: pp. 52 *cl*, 58 *r*, 59 *br*; The Edinburgh Photographic Library/David Morrison: pp. 38 *bl*, 39 *tr*; Chris Fairclough Colour Library: pp. 24 *tc*, 141 *tr*; Maggie Murray/Format Photographers: p. 121 *tl*; Sally and Richard Greenhill: p. 141 *cl*; Robert Harding Picture Library: pp. 85 *tl*, 128; Robert Harding Picture Library/Martyn F. Chillmaid: p. 24 *ml*; Robert Harding Picture Library/Rob Cousins: p. 101 *cl*; Hulton Deutsch Collection Limited: p. 140 *c*; The Image Bank: pp. 105 *c*, 120 *tl*; Images Colour Library: p. 140 *b*; Piers Cavendish/Impact Photos: p. 24 *mc*; John Hoffmann/Impact Photos: p. 121 *bl*; Andrew Littlejohn: pp. 120 *tr & bl*, 139 *r*; Nigel Luckhurst: pp. 7 *t*, 80 *ml & b*, 81 *t*, 139 *bl*; NHPA/Stephen Dalton: 46 *bl*; NHPA/Gerard Lacz: pp. 7 *br*; NHPA/Jany Savvanet: 52 *tl*; PA News: pp. 6 *bl*, 101 *b*; Photo Library International: pp. 100 *tcr*, 121 *tr*; Pictor International: pp. 62 *t*, 100 *tl & br*; Popperphoto: p. 140 *t*; Graham Portlock: pp. 6 *ml*, 7 *l*, 24 *b*, 33, 34, 44, 52 *b*, 56, 65, 66, 67, 68, 69, 72, 75, 80 *t & mr*, 81 *b* (with thanks to McLean Homes Ltd.), 95, 105 *r*, 115, 125 *l*, 132, 139 *tl*; Spectrum Colour Library: p. 39 *cl*; Tony Stone Images: pp. 45, 46 *tl, tc, tr, bcr & br*, 60, 100 *tr & bl*, 101 *t*, 109, 112; Topham Picturepoint: p. 120 *br*; Trip/Helene Rogers: p. 141 *br*.

t = top *m* = middle *b* = bottom *r* = right *c* = centre *l* = left

Picture research by Sandie Huskinson-Rolfe of PHOTOSEEKERS.

Cover illustration by Felicity Roma Bowers.
Cover design by Dunne & Scully.